3|2|

ALSO BY REBECCA CARROLL

Uncle Tom or New Negro?: African Americans Reflect on Booker T. Washington and Up from Slavery 100 Years Later (ed.)

Saving the Race: Conversations on Du Bois from a Collective Memoir of Souls

Sugar in the Raw: Voices of Young Black Girls in America

Swing Low: Black Men Writing

I Know What the Red Clay Looks Like: The Voice and Vision of Black Women Writers

Surviving the White Gaze

❧ A Memoir ❧

Rebecca Carroll

Simon & Schuster

New York   London   Toronto   Sydney   New Delhi

Simon & Schuster
1230 Avenue of the Americas
New York, NY 10020

First Simon & Schuster hardcover edition February 2021

SIMON & SCHUSTER and colophon are
registered trademarks of Simon & Schuster, Inc.

For information about special discounts for bulk purchases,
please contact Simon & Schuster Special Sales at 1-866-506-1949
or business@simonandschuster.com.

The Simon & Schuster Speakers Bureau can bring authors to your live event.
For more information or to book an event,
contact the Simon & Schuster Speakers Bureau at 1-866-248-3049
or visit our website at www.simonspeakers.com.

Interior design by Ruth Lee-Mui

Manufactured in the United States of America

1   3   5   7   9   10   8   6   4   2

Library of Congress Cataloging-in-Publication Data
Names: Carroll, Rebecca, author.
Title: Surviving the White Gaze : A Memoir / Rebecca Carroll.
Description: First Simon & Schuster hardcover edition. |
New York : Simon & Schuster, 2021. |
Identifiers: LCCN 2020029852 (print) | LCCN 2020029853 (ebook) |
ISBN 9781982116255 (hardcover) | ISBN 9781982116279 (paperback) |
ISBN 9781982116323 (ebook)
Subjects: LCSH: Carroll, Rebecca. | Interracial adoption—New Hampshire—Warner
(Town) | Adopted children—New Hampshire—Warner (Town)—Biography. | Race
awareness in children—New Hampshire—Warner (Town) | Racially mixed families—
New Hampshire—Warner (Town) | African American women authors—Biography. |
African Americans—Race identity.
Classification: LCC HV875.65.N47 C37 2021 (print) | LCC HV875.65.N47 (ebook) |
DDC 305.48/8960730092 [B]—dc23
LC record available at https://lccn.loc.gov/2020029852

ISBN 978-1-9821-1625-5
ISBN 978-1-9821-1632-3 (ebook)

For Kofi

Surviving the White Gaze

⚜ Prologue ⚜

When I was writing this book, I asked a few friends, family, and former students to share memories if they were inclined, from when we first met or of experiences that stood out for them. This note came from Felicia, who was among the handful of black students I had at an all-girls private school outside of Boston, where I taught ninth grade English and eleventh grade history for the 1995–1996 academic year, when I was twenty-five and she was sixteen.

There are gaps in my memory from my childhood. I can't tell you if this was my sophomore year or my junior year, but my memory of the first time meeting you is this: You asked us to write a memory from our summer. That summer was my first time being in jail. My paragraph or two recounted how I had run from the Boston Police after being tracked down for running away from home. I'm sure my classmates wrote of travels abroad or time with family and friends.

But mine was different. Home at that time was unbearable. I was unbearable. But you asked. And no one had ever cared to ask. And you looked like me. So I told you about how I had almost out run them, and then how my wrists were too small for the handcuffs after they caught me. I went to court and then to the foster home. But very neatly by the time school started, I was back home and in my private school and in your class. You were my first black teacher ever and you were the light.

This is what black folks are to one another—we are the light that affirms and illuminates ourselves *to* ourselves. A light that shines in its reflection of unbound blackness, brighter and beyond the white gaze. The path to fully understanding this, and my ultimate arrival at the complicated depths of my own blackness, was a decades-long, self-initiated rite of passage, wherein I both sought out and pushed away my reflection, listened to the wrong people, and harbored an overwhelming sense of convoluted grief—a grief that guided me here, to myself.

⚜ *One* ⚜

"I'm gonna put chocolate chips in mine," I chirped, scrambling to gather up a handful of small dark pebbles to mix into my mud pie. The mucky mound was fast losing its shape inside the long, narrow tire grooves of our dirt driveway, still wet from rain the day before. The sky was a faint azure blue, and the sweet, powdery fragrance of milkweed wafted in the distance. "And some sprinkles," I said, adding a few strands of freshly tugged grass from the lawn nearby, cool in my hand on a warm summer morning.

Leah, my best friend, barely looked up, so intently absorbed in the creation of her own mud pie, rounding it with her fingers to perfection. Even at four years old, she was detail-oriented and meticulous, a budding artist who took her work very seriously, while I at four had more of a collagist approach to things: the more elements and textures and ingredients, the better. When Leah was finished with her pie, she found a thin twig to outline a pattern on the top—not as simple as a plain lattice like the apple piecrusts Mom made, but tiny squares and triangles and circles interconnected, similar to a design in the pages of one of the thick art books lying around our house, and hers, too.

Leah's mom, Hannah, was a good friend of Mom and Dad. She had come over with Leah in the morning and visited with Mom for a little while as we played before doing some tai chi in the front yard. After a couple of hours, it was time to go. Leah and I hugged our goodbyes, her soft white wisp of a body fixed inside my bare brown arms, as the sun started to stretch high into the afternoon above the trees and beyond our wide-eyed, handmade world. "Bye!" we simultaneously trilled into each other's ears. "OK, girls," Hannah said, smiling at the closeness we'd nurtured from when we were babies lying on a blanket together, reaching for each other's fingertips. "We'll get together again soon, OK? Bye, Laurette!" Mom waved goodbye to Hannah and Leah from where she stood, leaning against the worn wooden doorjamb of our country farmhouse.

Warner, the New Hampshire town where we lived, had a population of approximately 1400 when we moved there in 1969, and I became its sole black resident. We rented our farmhouse from longtime Warner residents who owned a lot of land and property in town. The house sat on the top of a dirt road called Pumpkin Hill, which was lined up and down by a dilapidated stone wall of various-sized rocks and stones, leading into different parts of town on either side. There was a shed connected off the right of our house, and a giant freestanding barn to the left, separated from the house by the wide driveway where Leah and I had played that morning. An apple tree with rugged, splayed branches good for climbing stood planted squarely in the front yard. Not another house in sight, nor a neighbor within earshot.

After Leah went home, my sister, Riana, who at seven years old had already developed such a keen love for horses that it was almost all consuming, decided it was time to play her very favorite game, the "horse game." We made our horses out of chairs and used curtain sashes for reins. The solitary quiet of our house wrapped itself around our make-believe landscape so thoroughly that the damp dirt-and-honey scent of our horses filled the room.

We heard the gallop of their hooves, and felt the pace of their gait, posting to the trot, up and down in the smooth, hard dip of our saddles.

Born with two freckles above each nostril of her nose, Riana wore her shoulder-length hair tucked behind her ears as she led us along a winding outdoor trail. Our horses bucked and neighed as we gave their pretend bellies soft little heel kicks. Her posture was straight, almost rigid, as she sat high and proud in her saddle.

"Time to set up camp!" Riana said, her joy palpable as she pushed the walls beyond her old sisterless imagination into a reality with room for me inside.

We pulled the reins to a halt, hopped down and roped the horses to a tree, fed them hay, gave them water, and brushed out their manes.

"Let's build a fire here," she said, pointing to a small patch of rug near a standing jade plant tall enough to pose as a short tree, and then began to gather kindling from nearby.

I shadowed her movements and tried to match her focus.

Riana pretended to struggle to open a can of soup because we'd forgotten the can opener, so she had to use her Swiss Army knife instead, and finally managed to cut through the top of the can without hurting herself. She emptied the contents into the pot while I held it over the fire so we could get our dinner started. We ate our canned soup out of mugs, and then rolled out our imaginary sleeping bags. Riana pet the horses one last time before bed. "Good night, horses," she said, her hand so slight and careful, her voice an aria of innocence.

Our brother, Sean, older than Riana by just two years, had been playing outside all morning with his friend Charlie, building and crafting and exploring and climbing. Charlie was kind and funny, skinny and curious, with buck teeth and brown hair. He rode over on his bike from town, where he lived with his reputable, middle-class family in a decorous house on Main Street. He loved to climb the apple tree in our front yard and sit among the limbs looking out at the world around him, but came down to join Sean in working on his latest invention, a go-cart with coffee-can headlights and a dish-towel cover nailed to four pieces of balsa wood somehow affixed with duct tape to an old Radio Flyer wagon.

"You're welcome to stay for dinner," Mom said as Charlie hopped back onto his red ten-speed bike to head home not too long after he'd arrived.

"That's OK, I'll be back!" he said, with a wide grin, still high from his time in the apple tree. "The Carrolls' . . . ," he sang over his shoulder as his bike wheels turned over the dirt and pointed him down the hill toward town, "Where Kids are King!"

At three or four o'clock in the afternoon, we all broke from play to gather at the dining room table, covered with a turquoise-blue-and-white gingham tablecloth, set with four delicate matching teacups and saucers. Riana, Sean, and I waited for Mom to come in from the kitchen with a white ceramic teapot filled with piping-hot mint tea, and a plate of freshly baked hermit cookies, our favorite, with their buttery, chewy molasses-and-clove-sweetened goodness. The smell of them filled the room, and it felt like we were floating in an airy confection. I reached for a second hermit and then a third, my little brown fingers sticky from plucking out the soft, warm raisins and popping them into my mouth. Riana had just one, which she ate slowly and relished, and Sean had four, one right after the other.

"Tell me about your day," Mom said, sipping her tea, her long black hair pulled into a low ponytail folded up and pinned with a barrette at the back of her head. Slight of frame, modest by nature,

Mom was buoyant and tireless when it came to mothering us as young kids. While Dad taught art all day at a nearby private college, Mom stayed home with us, ever present, always with unwavering interest in our stories and questions, packing us into snowsuits in the winter, letting me and Riana run around topless in the summer, one creamy white chest, the other toasty brown.

She looped her fingers through the thin handle of her teacup and set it in its saucer to rest, smiling and ready to hear our stories.

"We made mud pies!" I squawked.

"And we played horses, too," Riana said, with gentle consternation, like the big sister she was, reminding me of the importance of our shared game, the game that she had herself devised and chose to include me in.

Sean was often quiet, until he wasn't. He teased me relentlessly starting when I was about six, and he began calling me a "hyper scale cow"—the name he came up with mainly because my skin was constantly dry and scaly. It looked like chalk dust in the winter, and could get silt-like in the summer. Nobody else in the family had need for daily use of moisturizing lotion, so there was never any in the house until I saw a commercial for Vaseline Intensive Care lotion in my early teens and bought myself a giant bottle from Cricenti's Market in town. When I first started to use it, I couldn't believe it had taken me so long to discover this magical cream that disappeared the dust and silt. The "hyper" and "cow" parts of the name were added because Sean thought I was too hyperactive and ate too much.

On this day, though, when we were still small and tender, Sean was quiet as we finished our hermits, and a tall standing lamp in the corner of the room carved a tiny patch of light as the day's natural light began to fade. "Thanks, Mom!" we said, nearly in unison, before leaping from the table to resume our play. Knowing our stations, easy with one another's company, sewing a fragile thread of siblinghood that we never imagined would fall apart.

At dinnertime, Dad and Mom carried the dining room table out the back door into the yard just outside the house. The table's four heavy wooden legs dug into the grass as Mom and Dad pushed them down farther into the pliant soil to keep the surface steady. With the vegetable garden at our backs, and the rusty but still functioning swing set off to the far side of the yard, we sat in mismatched chairs much less steady than the table, a family of five, together at the crowning moment of most summer days during our years on Pumpkin Hill, gloriously ravenous after a long day of play.

I had changed out of my play clothes and put on an olive green dress with black trim and white buttons down the front, one of a few frilly dresses that were handed down from friends, and which I alternated with the jumpers and tops that Mom made for me herself. Knees pulled up to my chest, I sat with bare feet, toes curled at the edge of my high chair, afro thick and wild, a coarse bunch of small snarls knotted and mangled like the yarn of a fumbled crochet project.

Riana sat to my left in a regular, grown-up chair, wearing a striped short-sleeve T-shirt and long pants. Shoulders slightly hunched now, not like when she was riding her pretend horse, and elbows on the table. Riana's facial expressions were always dreamy-eyed, a bit goofy, some mix of wistful and whimsical, as if she and she alone had just seen a monkey wearing diamond-studded sunglasses pull into the driveway behind the wheel of a regular old yellow school bus, and wasn't that kind of great? Maybe that monkey wanted to come play horses or hopscotch. Or maybe he was lost and didn't know how to find his way home.

Sean sat opposite Riana, facing the fields, with his straight brown hair in a bowl cut, cream-colored collared shirt from the thrift shop, and high-water corduroy pants. Not as hunched as Riana, but almost as dreamy-eyed, Sean looked beyond all of us into the early night, toward the border of the woods, yearning, I imagine, for the next time when he could pack up his tent, sleeping bag, canteen, and Sterno stove for another solo camping adventure.

Quiet but for our laughter and conversation, the field stretched behind us in a slow incline out and up where it crested to form a steep hill spread over with tall wheat stocks and patches of wild strawberries and wildflowers, a bouquet of which Mom had picked this morning and placed in a vase at the center of the dinner table. Mom served us steamed summer squash, fresh tomatoes with purple basil, and steamed pigweed, also known as lambsquarters, all from the garden, while Dad drank a tall glass mug of amber-colored Ballantine ale at the head of the table. Glints of peach-colored sunset bounced off our silverware, and the air was still enough for the flames of two long taper candles to grow brighter.

Cambrick, Riana's orange tabby she'd had since he was a kitten, sauntered up to the table from around the other side of the house, rubbed up against her legs dangling under the table, and then moved on. We had started out with two cats, Max and Sophie, and then Sophie had kittens, and her kittens grew up and had kittens, and at one point we had fourteen cats that all lived outside roaming the grounds, monitoring for field mice like slinky little feline sentinels. We gave most of them away, but were allowed to keep four or five, whom we gave names like Ocean Eyes and Butterscotch, Tiger and Teddy. Riana picked Cambrick early on as her own, and the two were constant companions, inasmuch as a cat is willing to be a companion.

Dad, at the head of the table, held up his glass of ale to make a toast, his bare arm pale and fleshy in a worn white cotton T-shirt, thick auburn hair past his ears and parted to one side, like a composer from the German Romantic era, and held down by a red terry cloth headband to keep it out of his eyes. I cupped my glass of milk with two hands; Riana and Sean held their glasses with one. Mom's skin shone warm in the last slivers of sunlight as she raised her glass, too, and we all clinked and some of my milk spilled, and our chairs wobbled in the grass, and we laughed.

"Look how lucky we all are," Dad said, his eyes ablaze with satisfaction. He looked at the garden, its tall stocks of corn to one end, neatly lined rows of tomato plants and green beans, thick, sprawling zucchini and summer squash vines, and then out toward the broad fields beyond. "Laurette, can you believe this?" Dad said, as if he couldn't believe it himself, that he'd really pulled it off and created a life that looked exactly the way he wanted it to look. Mom smiled, her face darling and spare, soft and unweathered.

"I know, Dave," she said. "It's beautiful. Just beautiful."

It *was* beautiful, and we *were* lucky. But beauty is subjective, and luck doesn't care about the choices other people make.

✢ Two ✢

I've known the story of my adoption from as far back as I can remember. "Tess and Roy were my high school students, but they were also my friends," Dad told me when I was very young.

Mom and Dad met at the Museum School in Boston, Massachusetts. Young and idealistic, both raised in strict, working-class, Catholic households, they married young and started a family right away. Dad took a job as an art teacher at a high school in Wolfeboro, New Hampshire, where they moved when Mom was very pregnant with Riana, and Sean was a toddler. An artist and naturalist, Dad was drawn to the undeveloped land and rural setting of Wolfeboro, which, like most of New Hampshire, was staunchly conservative—just a few decades later, businessman and Republican politician Mitt Romney would buy a summer residence there—and Kingswood High School, which had opened only a couple of years prior, was a rigid reflection of that.

In the late 1960s, as political unrest exploded all over the country, the Vietnam War raged on, and black America fought for basic civil rights, Dad set down roots in an all-white, provincial landscape for himself and his family, where he could pioneer his own brand of personal resistance.

Dad often mentioned his time at Kingswood, where he kept his classroom open to whomever, taught with an interpretive style, and always encouraged independent thinking. Students called him by his first name, as Riana, Sean, and I did for many years until I was the one to decide that we should call him Dad. He explained how he'd become a friend and ally to Roy and Tess, a rebellious and charismatic brother and sister, seventeen and sixteen, respectively, when they enrolled at Kingswood the same year he started teaching, also newly relocated to New Hampshire from Boston.

Dad said Tess and Roy's parents had divorced, and their mother, Lena, had been diagnosed with schizophrenia and abruptly institutionalized, while their father, George, had little to no paternal instincts, Roy had told him. Tess and Roy had come to live with Frances, their maternal grandmother, at the home where Frances had raised Lena in southern New Hampshire.

Dad said Tess and Roy found comfort and camaraderie in the family he was making with Mom, and often visited their house for dinner and lively conversation, with Sean underfoot and baby Riana on Mom's hip.

Not long into the school year, Tess discovered she'd gotten pregnant during one of her trips back to Boston to see her boyfriend, an older black man. Tess dropped out of school to figure out her options, but on her last day before leaving she left a letter in Dad's office mailbox, explaining her situation. In that letter, Dad explained, he saw an opportunity that he thought might work for everyone.

"We had Sean and Riana, and we wanted another child," he told me. "But we believed in Zero Population Growth, and so we didn't want to bring another child into the world and all."

From the very beginning, Dad described a situation free of tension, even for the teenage girl, a student he had mentored, who had gotten pregnant and was not prepared to become a mother.

"So I called Tess, and told her that if she was interested, we would be willing to adopt her baby," as Dad's story goes. "It wasn't a problem that the father was black. In fact," he said, "if anything, the idea of adopting a child of another race had great appeal for us. We had thought about adopting a Native American child, but I think there was a real problem with placing Native Americans at that time."

Dad has always boasted about having an innate connection to Native Americans based on his own reverence for and spiritual connection to the natural world, his passion for preserving wildlife, and his devout anti-commercial-development stance.

I was told that my birth father was black, but that was all I knew about him. Mom and Dad never spoke his name or told me where he was from, where he was now, or what his feelings were about me or about Tess. Nothing beyond the fact that he was black, and that Tess had decided he would not be part of whatever her plans might be regarding my upbringing. Mom and Dad didn't have pictures of either biological parent, but the absence of information about my birth father, and the fact that my parents had not had any sort of relationship or interaction with him when they were negotiating my adoption, made him seem less important in the overall retelling of my story.

We didn't watch much TV as kids. For a long time we didn't even have a TV. But when we finally got one, an old black-and-white Zenith, I remember seeing Easy Reader for the first time on the classic children's PBS show *Electric Company*, and immediately imagining that he could be my birth father. I'd watch eagerly as a young Morgan Freeman sang about words and reading, with his perfectly rounded afro, black turtlenecks, and cool '70s sunglasses, feeling an inexplicable connection, as if he saw me as sure as I saw him. His dark skin mixed with my white birth mother's skin would account for the lighter brown shade of my own skin, which I'd heard the adults around me describe as "beautiful" or "mocha-colored," as if it were a shade I'd picked out myself as part of my personal style, an accessory like the scarves and jewelry and puffy-sleeved blouses that I'd become known for mixing and matching in various forms.

And then, when *The Electric Company* was over, so, too, was the imagining.

"I tried to talk her out of it," Mom's version of my adoption story always begins. "We went for a long walk behind the house, Tess and I, and I really played devil's advocate with her. I told her she could do it, she could keep you."

Raised in the New Hampshire coastal town of Portsmouth, where her father worked as a naval pilot, Mom can appear fragile, but she is adamant about some things. "The most defiant person I know," Dad likes to say about her, although I've never seen her this way. Someone who aggressively yearns for everything and everyone to be OK, Mom went to art school despite the objections of her parents, but majored in commercial art to placate them. She switched to drawing after her first year, when she met Dad, who cast such a spell that she called off an engagement to a man her parents had approved of, but whom she'd suspected was gay. Mom married Dad in the same local church where she'd spent hundreds of Sundays quietly bored out of her mind, in a proper white veil and gown, as a final gesture of appeasement to her parents.

After they were married, free to sate their own desires and cultivate their own ideals, Mom and Dad decided that the family they would make together would be free of rules and religion, rich with art and laughter no matter how little money they had, each person an individual of his or her own making. Like "pre-Garibaldi

Italy," as Dad described it. "A loose federation of independent city states."

No angry, violent rages or lamps thrown across the room, as there had been in Dad's own childhood in southeastern Connecticut. No terrifying car trips in the pitch-dark night with a blind-drunk parent behind the wheel. No church on Sunday or any other day of the week, no family dinners or duties or obligations. Nobody counting the empty liquor bottles in the trash cans outside or telling anyone they'd burn in hell for using the Lord's name in vain. No Ecclesiastes or Blood of Christ. No sin. No guilt.

At first, Tess accepted Dad's offer, the choice her brother, Roy, had encouraged, I was told, and when Mom felt she'd made her best effort to talk Tess out of keeping me, she was committed. But soon after I was born, Tess changed her mind.

"Mom was crushed," Dad said. "But we knew it was a possibility, and we tried to understand."

Three weeks later, Tess changed her mind again, and I became part of the Carroll family—a verbal agreement that did not become legal for three years, when Mom finally insisted on it, anxious that Tess would change her mind yet again and come back for me.

Tess later got her GED, a term that meant nothing to me as a child, but that Dad said allowed her to go to college, get an education, and move on with her life. Beyond that, I only knew that one day, when the time was right, it would be arranged for us to meet. I was desperate for the time to be right. The idea of her loomed large as the central character in a fairy tale written just for me, and I lived somewhere in between faith in her existence and disquiet over the lack of any proof beyond the story my parents told me.

✣ Three ✣

I skipped around the living room as the evening started to set outside, wearing a bright peacock blue long-sleeve shirt with white underpants, little bare legs Tootsie Roll brown and chubby. Mom wore a snug yellow-ocher turtleneck, a brown knee-length skirt, and tights as she busied herself setting up chairs she'd brought in from the kitchen and a folding table with a fresh, floral-print tablecloth for food and beverages. She put out chips and onion dip, and parsley meatballs with toothpicks, punch and cocktail makings, stacks of paper plates and a tower of clear plastic cups.

The three of us kids were allowed to stay up for the grown-up party if we wanted, even though no other kids were coming. Sean and Riana decided to go to bed and were already fast asleep as guests began to arrive, but I couldn't wait—never wanting to miss an opportunity to twirl and shine, use my big words and listen to adults use even bigger ones.

I grinned, tippy-toeing on bare feet from grown-up to grown-up, lifting myself closer to their gaze, stopping to slip my hand inside the hand of tall, quiet Olive, who had been in Mom and Dad's life forever. Elegant with short, set hair and romantic eyes, Olive brimmed with benevolence as she clasped her long, cool fingers around my little palm. She looked down at me and smiled.

"You look so pretty, Becky," Olive said, her voice silvery and melodic. "What a big girl you are to stay up so late." Her partner, Tina, boisterous and brassy, stood a few feet behind, where we could hear her laughing loudly with other guests.

"Are you working on any new plays?" Olive asked. "That one you performed the last time I visited was wonderful!"

"Yes!" I said, before bounding off through the knot of kneecaps and noise.

Hannah, Leah's mom and Mom's good friend, came with her husband, Ezra, wearing a stylish leather jacket and the same kind of pants she wore when she did tai chi in our front yard, high-waisted and bell-bottomed, in a faded red corduroy. Her jet-black bangs hung just above her eyebrows, and long silver earrings dangled from her earlobes. Ezra rarely visited, and mostly kept to himself, so it was a surprise to see him. I hugged them both, and Hannah knelt down to tenderly cup my face in her hands.

"How are you doing?" she asked, with a look of both marvel and concern.

"I'm great!" I said, my cheeks bursting.

The room filled up fast, and soon I couldn't see where Mom was among the crowd of adults exchanging small talk, dipping their chips, and filling their glasses with punch. Dad had disappeared early on, after I'd seen him greet a woman I recognized from the weekly drawing group he and Mom were part of that gathered every Friday afternoon at a different house.

"There's my little wifey," I heard a familiar voice say from behind me. John was a close family friend who visited often, and regularly celebrated holidays with us. He had beady eyes, and his hands were weirdly oversized, with bulging veins that stuck out and wiggled under his skin. John told us that one of the bigger veins was a worm he'd swallowed as a child. Often, when he came to visit for a couple of days, he'd stay up late and tell us scary stories into the night—sometimes with all three of us, other times with just me and Riana. He was a masterful storyteller and made up the most memorable characters, like the wolfman with sharp teeth and bloody human fingers, or the sleek red fox who loved the moon and cried into his evening bowl of porridge.

John was fond of Sean and Riana, but he was especially fond of me, and took to calling me his "wifey" because, he said, I was his special girl, and we could pretend to be husband and wife.

He crouched down now and put his hands around my five-year-old waist, his pointy nose so close I could see the wiry hairs inside his nostrils. "How's my wifey tonight?"

John's hands slid down around my hips.

"Hi, John," I said, feeling better to be talking to someone I knew, even though his breath smelled terrible. "Do you know where my mom is?"

John stood up, moving his thick hands to hold onto my shoulders. He looked around and then knelt back down, at eye level with me again, teeth huge under his tight, wide lips. I started to feel squeamish thinking about how easily his hands could cover so much of my body, as if they could slide the skin off my bones if he wanted them to. He had touched me before in the daylight, or after dinner during story time, his hand grazing my thigh or a finger tickling my neck. Tonight, though, it felt like he was holding on to me too tightly, and I didn't understand why or whether that was something a grown-up man should be doing to a little girl.

"I don't see her," he said. "Maybe she's in the kitchen?" I sidled out from under his hands, feeling a little faint and panicky. Wading through grown-up bodies from the waist down, I saw a pair of legs wearing the same colored tights I remembered Mom was wearing, and threw my arms around them, only to look up and see it wasn't Mom at all.

I didn't know who the woman was whose legs I mistook for Mom's, but she picked me up right away, seeing the worried and frightened look on my face, and carried me into the kitchen, where Mom was refilling the chip bowl. "Hi, Laurette, I think this little one is looking for you." She handed me to Mom, who took me in her arms, setting my legs to wrap around her waist.

"I'm right here, Becky. Don't worry," she said, hugging me tight. "Remember I love you so much." Mom kept me on her hip as she brought the chip bowl back out to the party. I was safe on her hip, in her arms, safe inside the bubble that was our house on Pumpkin Hill. I had no idea how spectacularly that bubble would eventually burst.

✦ Four ✦

We had neighbors for the first time after we moved to our new house when I was six, and Nicole, a girl my age with freckled cheeks and caramel-colored hair, lived right next door. We sat together at the giant table in the dining room of her house one afternoon, surrounded by fancy lamps of varying sizes and styles, some attached to the wall, others resting on smooth side tables, crystal goblets behind glass in a stand-alone cupboard, and upholstered chairs set against the walls without purpose.

Nan, Nicole's mom, served us chicken noodle soup in delicate, unchipped bowls along with perfectly shaped spoons, silver and shiny. Apple juice hit just above the halfway mark in thick, squat ornamental glasses, and I felt hesitant to take a sip, worried I might spill on the neatly embroidered placemats under our soup bowls.

Nicole, all cheeks and pink lips, both free-spirited and polite, ate her soup with abandon, but used her napkin carefully, dabbing at her mouth after a spoonful of noodles. "You should come!" she said, before lifting her glass of juice and gulping it down so fast I thought maybe she hadn't had anything to drink in months.

"Come where?" I asked.

"To ballet!" Nicole said, as if it were talking about something magical.

"I'll tell your mother about it," said Nan, who appeared out of nowhere in tennis whites, her crisp blonde hair short, and shaped close around her tanned face. "Now, Nic," Nan said, directing her attention at Nicole, "Daddy has an auction and I'm going to go play tennis with Ann. But first we need to pick up your little brother from soccer, so let's finish up your lunch and we'll drive Becky home, OK?"

"OK, Mom. But remember to tell Becky's mom about ballet, OK?" Nicole said, seeming very pleased with herself.

"I will," Nan said, suddenly rushing around behind us, gathering up sweatshirts and a change of sneakers, putting sandwiches with cut crust in plastic bags and packing everything inside two separate canvas totes. "I think Mrs. Rowland would be great for Becky to learn from," Nan's voice sounded different when she said this, tense and hurried, and I wondered if it was because she was out of breath from all her sudden movement.

"Is Mrs. Rowland your ballet teacher?" I asked Nicole.

"Yep, and she's really nice," Nicole answered, pushing back from the table, leaving her empty bowl and juice glass on her placemat. "You can leave your bowl and stuff there, our cleaning lady will do it."

"Come on, girls," Nan said, starting to grow impatient, even though we'd only just finished eating.

We piled into Nan's Volvo and drove the short distance to my house. I hopped out of the car, and Nan rolled down her window to talk to Mom, who greeted us in the driveway.

"I was telling Becky about Nicole's ballet class," Nan said.

"No, Mommy, *I* was telling Becky about my ballet class," Nicole chimed in from the back seat.

"OK, Nic, let me talk to Becky's mom now." Nan 's lips were naturally pursed, but seemed more so now, as if sharing this information was an inelegant chore. "Mrs. Rowland teaches out of her studio in New London. You know where New London is, right?" Nan said this as if we'd just moved to Warner from outer space, instead of the three miles from our house on Pumpkin Hill.

Yes," Mom said, clearly still trying to negotiate the reality of having neighbors. She looked almost as if she'd been ambushed.

"My Nicole really likes the teacher," Nan said. "OK! We've got to be off, let me know if you'd like more information about the classes, Laurette. I think you'll want to send her." Nan gave Mom a tight smile before backing out of the driveway while Nicole waved at me through the window.

"Would you like to go to a ballet class, Beck?" Mom said, looking down at me, her arm around my shoulder as I leaned into her hip.

"Yes!" I said, breaking from her to spin and cartwheel across the driveway, while Mom watched and smiled, her laser-focused love like a spotlight on my impromptu performance.

Later that afternoon, I overheard Mom on the phone. "Oh, I see," Mom said. "Thanks, Nan, I can see why you think this ballet class would be so good for Becky. Mm-hmm, right. And thank you for offering to give her a ride."

I started to imagine being a ballerina, not fully understanding how ballet was different from other kinds of dancing, but eager to participate in another form of creative expression. I had already written plays and stories and created elaborate worlds, both material and imagined, and now I was going to be a ballerina!

Mom didn't get her driver's license until she was thirty-six, four years later, and Dad was busy working, so I got a ride to my first ballet class with Nan and Nicole.

On the fifteen-mile car ride to New London, where the dance

school was, I sat with Nicole in the back seat of Nan's Volvo, squirming with excitement as it purred along the highway. A stiff, clean canvas tote like I'd seen Nan pack after lunch the week before, but this one with red handles and the L.L.Bean label, sat between us, with Nicole's pink ballet slippers, a small Holly Hobbie thermos, and Hunt's Snack Pack chocolate pudding inside. I didn't have a snack, but even more than the pudding, I envied Nicole's Holly Hobbie thermos. Holly Hobbie with her little blonde braids, peachy skin, and patchwork dress, single thread of a smile and big brown eyes. Nan occasionally looked back at us in the rearview mirror, her eyebrows almost as white as her teeth.

The studio was spacious, with a linoleum floor, ceiling lights, wall-to-wall mirrors, and bars running the length of one side of the room. It felt somehow glamorous, stagelike, and important. Girls gathered in a room off the main studio to change out of their shoes and into their slippers, while I just stood in the doorway of the studio taking it all in, eager and fluttery, immediately dreaming about performing in front of giant audiences, taking numerous bows and returning for encores, flowers pouring onto the stage from fans.

She appeared suddenly, like a stencil cutout in the left corner of my eye. A one-dimensional, dark silhouette bending and arching without a face. An abstract image, gradually taking the shape of a head, attached to a long, giraffe-like neck and body. This inky-colored figure from afar didn't look like anything or anyone in the books I read, the dolls I played with, the people in my school, or the people in my family. And yet there was something familiar about her. It felt momentarily like being in a fog, but soon I could make out the tight curls of her afro, like tiny black jewels embedded in an even blacker crown.

When she turned toward me, the white of her eyes was dazzling, almost fluorescent set against the bare, brown-skinned beauty of her face. Her smile seemed as wide as my six-year-old wingspan, the full vision of her now walking across the studio floor.

"And who is this?" she said, extending her large, graceful hand.

"I'm Becky," I said, giving her a good shake.

"What a firm grip! Welcome to class, Becky," she said. "I'm Dede Rowland."

My ballet teacher was black. The first black person I had ever seen in real life. Was she real? Did she know Easy Reader from *The Electric Company*? Did she go home at night to live inside the TV with him and the words and letters he carried around with him in the pockets of his jacket?

Mrs. Rowland turned to get the attention of the rest of the other girls, all white, as were all the students in my elementary school. I had only known being the only black kid or person anywhere until this moment, when Mrs. Rowland made me one of two. "Girls! Let's get started at the bar. First position!" Mrs. Rowland demonstrated in the center of the room, her toes pointing straight through from her heels to form a V shape.

We practiced first through fifth of feet and arm positions, then *pliés* and a round of *relevés*. About halfway through class, we'd already finished one series of *grand jetés* when I stepped up to take my turn again to fly across the room.

"You already had a turn," one girl said, with her slender cap-sleeved arms crossed tightly over her flat, preadolescent chest, sleek brown hair pulled into a neat, high ponytail. "You can't just go again, you have to stand in line."

I was standing in line, I told her.

"You haven't even been here before. You can't just come in and take over the class and go first every time." How was I taking over the class? I wondered. Was I taking over the class?

"Girls!" Mrs. Rowland said, her voice slightly raised. "Everybody quiet now. Let's go back to the bar for some *rond de jambes.*" I turned back toward the bar and saw the girl who told me I was skipping the line lean in, whispering something to one of the other girls. They looked at me and laughed. I tried to make eye contact with Nicole, who turned away.

"Come on, girls! Let's go!" The music came back on, and we each assumed first position, then extended one leg forward, toe set to mark the beginning point before circling outward to the side, and back through first position to complete a *rond de jambe.*

"Very nice, girls," Mrs. Rowland said.

After class when I got home, I was telling Mom about how much fun I'd had, and she gently interrupted me. "And isn't it nice that Mrs. Rowland is black?" I paused for a minute.

"Oh, yeah," I said. Somehow hearing Mom say the word "black" took me off guard, and I got lost in a sudden reverie of questions. Why did Mom bring it up? Could *I* be related to Mrs. Rowland? Had I ever even heard Mom use the word "black" to refer to a person before? Did Mom like black people? Would I go live with Mrs. Rowland now?

Over the course of my lessons, I would learn that Mrs. Rowland had three children of her own—two boys in high school and a girl, Everly, who was two or three years ahead of me and in her mother's class for older girls, where she was also the only black student. We would occasionally cross paths in the studio, which was across the driveway from their house, or I might see the two boys in the front yard after class. Everly wore her hair long and straightened, styled with barrettes or bows, in ponytails and buns, like the white girls did. The boys wore big afros like Easy Reader, and gave off the same kind of coolness that felt both confusing and alluring. The Rowlands were a black family, and mine was not.

I could somewhat grasp that my ballet classes with Mrs. Rowland were a way to expose me to another black person, but without any further explanation or context, I still felt other, even if it was a very case-specific kind of othering. In my world my blackness made me feel special and treasured, but it didn't seem that was the case for Mrs. Rowland.

White mothers often dropped off their girls for class without making eye contact with her, and sometimes spoke to her in a dismissive manner. The Rowland family existed outside the realm of Mom and Dad's life and lens, and after Mom's initial comment about Mrs. Rowland being black, the issue never came up again. As if a box had been checked and Mom's work had been done. Every Thursday afternoon after I left class, I came home to a family and a world of whiteness, a world where no other black people ever entered besides me.

I studied ballet with Mrs. Rowland for five years, and often in her company, I felt small pangs of fragile awareness regarding who I might be, what my skin color might mean. There were days when I wanted to be, or believed I was, black just like Mrs. Rowland, but it also seemed as though I would have to give something up in order for that to remain true. Cocooned within a whiteness where my brown skin was mocha-colored, I spoke with an inflection similar to that of my white brother and sister, and my adult guardians were welcomed and centered wherever we went. I was being ushered through my life via the powerful passport of white privilege.

It didn't appear that Mrs. Rowland had that same access, and although she never seemed lonely or bitter, I at six and seven and eight years old simply could not imagine being out in the world as a black girl or black woman, as Mrs. Rowland was, without the benefits afforded by white stewardship—without my family. But I also couldn't deny how it felt when Mrs. Rowland saw me in ways that my parents could not, or did not.

Mrs. Rowland often made cameos in our seasonal recitals, which were always my favorite moments in the show, even more so than my own turn to perform. I loved to watch her dance. She commanded the stage and the audience, whether she was dancing to *Rhapsody in Blue* or something from the *Nutcracker* Suite, her torso an anchor of moving parts, waving and jutting and looping. There was so much power and love in her movement, so much dedication and range. And she absolutely exuded joy.

When I could, I'd watch her perform from the curtain wings and wait for her to finish, when she'd exit the stage and rush off to a costume change or some other recital demand, but not before giving me a quick, tight hug, looking me squarely in the eyes, her face agleam with a thin layer of sweat, lucent eyes and full lips, backlit by the dim transition lights set in between numbers, and nodding her head assuredly to acknowledge me in a way that defied words.

Makeup looked different on brown skin than it did on the white girls, and Mrs. Rowland brought her own for herself, and to share with her daughter and me. A lipstick or a blush that worked best on our particular skin tones. She always found ways to celebrate or emphasize my hair, which was generally a mess, by suggesting a crown or colorful scarves as part of my costumes. When we performed a stage version of *The Wiz*, she cast me in the role of the scarecrow, which had been played by Michael Jackson, whom I secretly loved, in the film version. Mrs. Rowland suggested a straw hat with wheat sticking out, which also served as a way to affix the hat to my afro so that it would stay on during my performance.

My relationship with Mrs. Rowland inspired me, in part, to write my very first essay. I had been encouraged by Dad to keep a journal, as he did, but meeting Mrs. Rowland led most pointedly to my discovery that writing could be a way to figure things out, or at least to write them into existence. One afternoon during my first year of ballet lessons, I found a piece of yellow-lined paper and a pencil in the drawing supply closet in our living room, and sat in the kitchen at the dinner table—the same one Mom and Dad used to carry out to the yard behind the house on the hill to eat our suppers outside—and wrote: *My name is Rebecca Anne Carroll. I am a black child.*

Five

Anita was the second black person I ever met in real life. She was from Massachusetts, and a longtime friend of Leah's parents, Hannah and Ezra. Anita wore her hair short and natural, and held beams of brightness in her eyes. She tried to teach me and Leah to dance the day I first met her at Leah's house. We were probably eight or nine years old, and could not stop laughing our way through Anita's instructions, which were both firm and generous.

"It's a very easy dance, you two. It's called the Bus Stop," she said, showing us the moves as she kicked one heel out in front of her, then to the side, before taking a few measured steps in both directions, her arms in matching motion. Leah and I watched, and tried to mimic her movements. Even though I had been taking ballet lessons for three years at that point, watching Anita dance, her round body fluid, at spectacular ease, less practiced and formal than Mrs. Rowland's, felt like a revelation.

"Y'all have two left feet!" Anita broke into uproarious laughter. Gradually Leah and I started to really focus, feel the beat, and there we were, a trio of Anita, Leah, and me—shuffling to the left, to the front, to the right, all in unison.

"We got it!" Leah and I kept dancing while Anita cheered us on.

When it was time for me to go home that day, Anita gave me a big hug, even though we'd only just met. I leaned into her willingness to hold me as she gently ran the smooth of her palm across my cheek, up to my hairline and over my hair, which she drew into her as close as the rest of me. She didn't pat my hair like most of the white adults in my life had; she hugged my hair with a palpable sense of loving familiarity.

Like mine, Leah's parents were artists, but Hannah and her husband, Ezra, were more sophisticated and modern in their artistry. They'd gone to RISD (Rhode Island School of Design), the prestigious Ivy League art school of art schools, and they were politically savvy and culturally sophisticated in a way that my parents were not. Ezra was a glassblower, and Hannah, a textile artist. Together, they made and sold Ezra's exquisite beaded glass necklaces, goblets, and tumblers for hundreds of dollars at seasonal craft shows around the country.

They also spent part of every summer on Martha's Vineyard, where Leah's grandmother owned a summer house, and had elaborate Hanukkah and Christmas celebrations that always included expensive gifts from Leah's uncle, a successful housewares distributor in Washington, DC. I was endlessly envious of those gifts. One year it was a VCR before anyone else in town had one. Another year ski equipment arrived for everyone in the family, which included Leah's two younger sisters.

Their house, with its big black potbelly stove and deep farmhouse sinks in the kitchen, narrow stairwells and dark back rooms, was marvelous to me. There were bowls of blown-glass marbles everywhere, random skeins of multicolored yarn and different metals and gems nestled in corners and random surfaces. It was an interior world that felt like being inside an actual piece of art, like the work of Friedensreich Hundertwasser, whose bold and brightly hued, spiral-influenced art was laid out in books big and small spread throughout their house. I loved Leah's house so much that one time I stole a can of tuna fish from their pantry. "I just wanted something from their house," I lamented when Mom discovered what I'd done.

One afternoon a few weeks after Anita taught us the Bus Stop, Leah and I were alone in her house while her parents worked in Ezra's glassblowing studio, about a hundred feet up the driveway. We'd finished taking turns reading aloud to each other from *Are You There God? It's Me, Margaret* by Judy Blume, and chanted our mantra from the book: "We must, we must, we must increase our bust!" Snooping around out of boredom and curiosity in the doorless connecting bedrooms upstairs, we discovered her father's stack of *Playboy* and *Penthouse* magazines under a bunch of other magazines and books in her parents' room.

Leah and I sat together on the floor with our backs pressed against Leah's bed, opposite the crib that her youngest sister still slept in, knees bent and bums touching, as we flipped through the pages of *Playboy*, eyes glued to image after image of naked women in various poses. We paused at one shot of a woman sitting with her legs spread, and tried to make out her vagina under its giant tangle of pubic hair.

"Our vaginas don't look like that," I said.

"Because we're little," Leah said, her eyes the shape of almonds, lips thin and girlish. "We don't have hair down there yet."

"Do you think we should look?" I asked. "To see if any hair has grown today?"

"Maybe later," Leah countered. "We should probably put these back before my parents come inside."

"But what do you think that cartoon meant about vagina's smelling like a skunk?" I asked as we stood up together to put the magazines back on the floor in her parents' room where we'd found them.

"I don't know, but my vagina doesn't smell like a skunk. Does yours?" Leah said, now on our way down the narrow, dark stairwell that led into the kitchen. "Wanna play I Want or Mon-Oh-Poly?"

I Want was a game we played by flipping through Hannah's issues of *Vogue* or the various department store catalogs she received in the mail, and taking turns pointing to one thing we were allotted to choose per page. We used the name Mon-Oh-Poly for another game we made up in which we pretended to be grown-ups with husbands and fancy clothes and cars and jobs.

"Let's make our houses today," I said.

One of my favorite things to do with Leah was to tear off giant pieces of paper from the tall utility rolls her parents had for packing their glasswork and draw blueprints for our dream houses, with detailed interior design for each room and the two-car garages we imagined we'd have. After we tore off our blank paper to work with, we pulled bins of glitter and glue, markers and buttons, tape and pipe cleaners from a row of shelves against the wall between the kitchen and the living room in Leah's house. And then we'd spread everything out on the floor and work for hours. Sometimes we'd tear another piece of paper off that we'd use to draw out the roads between that connected our houses.

"What do you think of a gold bathtub?" I asked.

"Seems a little much," Leah said without looking up, her hands as careful as I remembered them from that day from years before when we made mud pies in the driveway on Pumpkin Hill.

"I'm going to make an extra room for my biological mother so she has a place to stay when I finally meet her and she comes to visit me."

"That's gonna be so neat," Leah said cheerfully. "I wish you knew her already, because she's probably really nice."

"I sometimes don't know if I'm really going to meet her," I said, gluing some red glitter to the sides of my gold bathtub.

"Why not?" Leah looked up now, suddenly concerned for me, instinctively protective, as she'd always been. Her shiny brown hair was parted in the center, braided into two neat ponytails.

"Mom and Dave don't know when she'll be ready."

"Don't worry, Beck. Let's keep working, OK?"

"OK," I said, and we smiled at each other before putting our heads back down to create our worlds—worlds that felt as if they would be forever connected.

Six

Every year, from as far back as I can remember, Roy came to visit, usually during the summer so that he could play Wiffle ball with Dad. I knew that Roy was Tess's brother, which made him my uncle, but I never talked with him about this, because he seemed impossible to talk with about anything.

Blunt and loud, frenetic and opinionated, Roy concluded everything he said with a round summation—women shouldn't wear makeup, middle-class values are evil, marriage is provincial. He and Dad struck a feverish tenor from the moment Roy stepped in the door, like competitive scholars each trying to make the case for his better dissertation on the anti-intellectual roots of Dutch Calvinism or the liberation of cultural imperialism.

It wasn't until I was sixteen years old that I found the full-throated courage to confront him, even if it was in a letter and not to his face. I wrote:

> *You never listen to me or let me talk. And why are you constantly telling me how self-absorbed I am? Doesn't it make me more self-absorbed by focusing on it?*

He wrote back:

*As for letting other people talk——I am a blatant ageist, as well as a fast
listener. I do interrupt and have never felt that any 16-year-old was
nearly as interesting as I am, or has as much to offer conversationally.
Naturally, this is frustrating, at times, to energetic youth. . . . Regarding
self-absorption: since you posed the question——I do think it is the
Number One cause of most men disliking most women. Girls from
12–23 do tend toward it, rather than cultivating the world, they
cultivate a mirror, so to speak. I think you're susceptible——and I do kid
you about it.*

But in the years before, I kept my distance, straight up until
the time he brought his girlfriend, Claire, along with him for his
annual summer visit, when I was ten. Claire was tall and wil-
lowy, with soft brown eyes and round, plummy cheeks. Easy to
approach, with an almost angelic, Glinda the Good Witch voice
and presence. The complete opposite of Roy. After lunch, she and
I took a walk out to the two big gardens behind our house. Mom
and Dad had planted and grown large gardens here, as they had
behind the house on Pumpkin Hill, and in late summer, they were
teeming with vegetables and flowers—tomatoes and green beans,
zucchini and summer squash, sunflowers and peonies, poppies and
tulips.

Claire and I strolled the wide, grassy path together, passing
the compost pile on the right midway to the gardens. Claire told
me she worked as a social worker with kids and families back in
Portsmouth, New Hampshire, where she and Roy lived together. I
shared with her that I liked ballet and other kinds of dancing, and
sometimes reading, but mostly I liked watching TV and going to the
movies. But something else was on my mind as we approached the

first garden off the path, opposite the clothing line that hung the length between a tall pine tree and the old, dilapidated corn crib.

Roy and Claire had arrived in a yellowish, beat-up Chevy Nova with two empty car seats in the back. This was a different car from the one Roy usually drove to visit us in. Not that I paid such careful attention to the car he drove, but he'd come every year, and this time I couldn't help but notice the car seats because I knew that Roy didn't have kids. Maybe they'd given a ride to some friends who had kids?

Claire had been so easy to talk with from the moment we met that I felt comfortable asking her about the car seats. "Oh," she said, "we borrowed this car from Roy's sister, Tess.

"Tess is a good friend of mine. We were even roommates for a while before Roy and I got together," she said, smiling at the distant memory.

We paused at the foot of the garden, where all the large-petaled pink peonies were in their heaviest concentration. I felt like leaning my back into them, like a trust fall. How many times had I smelled them adoringly, or played and danced near them as Mom carefully pulled up the weeds around their roots. Would they catch me? Would anything or anyone catch me inside of this moment? Maybe I could lean forward into Claire, her naivete so resolute. Or would she need me to hold the weight of us both when I told her that her former college roommate, her boyfriend's sister, was my birth mother?

How did she not know who I was? Maybe she did know, and was just pretending she didn't to protect Tess's privacy?

"Did you know that Tess is my birth mother?" I asked, suddenly desperate to be proven wrong.

Claire's eyes softened, and her lips turned up into a delicate smile.

"No," she said. "I didn't." The sky spread out above us in aching silence.

I skipped straight from feeling hidden to feeling replaced.

"So those car seats are for . . . her kids?"

Claire's body shifted into a more professional posture, like Dr. Levis, our local doctor down the road, who smelled like formaldehyde and always bent toward me just slightly before she spoke, as if I were hard of hearing. "Yes," Claire said. "She has two beautiful baby boys."

"Do you think she thinks about me?" I blurted out before even fully processing what she had just told me. It was the question I'd wanted to ask Roy every single year since he had started visiting and I was old enough to know who he was, but hadn't had the courage.

"I'm sure she does," Claire said, her voice measured and compassionate.

"I don't think she wants to meet me," I said, eyes downcast, because if she did, why would she have had other children to replace me?

"I don't think that's true at all, Becky," Claire said. "I think she's probably very busy with two babies, but I'm sure she'd love to meet you."

I could hardly believe my birth mother had two kids. How was it possible that she had given me up, but kept two other kids? These were, then, my brothers? Would my having other siblings mean Riana and Sean would no longer be my brother and sister? Or would my new brothers be their new brothers, too? Tess, I thought, must love them so much more than she loved me, because she kept them. After eleven years of being a little sister, would I even know how to be a big sister? This all felt both revelatory and debilitating, like finding out you suddenly have superpowers, but can only use them if you throw away the thing in your life that makes you feel safest.

It suddenly clicked in my head that Roy had not told Claire about me because it must have been a secret he'd promised to keep—that *I* was a secret he'd promised to keep. The idea of being a secret ran so counter to everything I understood or felt myself to be, an outgoing, social, and inescapably *disclosed* entity. You couldn't miss me in my family if you tried, in my town, in my school, much less keep me a secret. It felt like further assurance that Tess didn't want to meet me.

Years later, Roy confirmed to me that he had in fact vowed to Tess he would protect this very private moment of her life from public knowledge, but it seemed unfair then that he had kept information about Tess from me while sharing information about me with her. The image of Tess that I had in my mind was frozen in time, the way she had been described to me by Dad, as a young, attractive, and precocious teenager with long brown hair and sometimes glasses. I could not comprehend the difference between seventeen-year-old Tess and the now twenty-seven-year-old Tess.

"She lives in Portsmouth, with her partner, Miguel," Claire said.

Somehow I understood that this was not my birth father, that my new brothers and I had different fathers, because Claire didn't mention my birth father at all. And how could Tess live so close for all these years without me knowing? I always imagined she lived in Boston, where she was from. But in Portsmouth of all places? A mere sixty-five miles away?

We visited Mom's parents, my grandparents, in Portsmouth every year a few days before Christmas, but no one had ever told me that Tess lived in the same town. While I was opening the inevitable, high-collared flannel nightgown wrapped in Christmas paper dotted with fat Santas, Tess could have been within walking distance, at her home reading bedtime stories to her babies, my brothers. Mom and Dad had always been transparent about everything, maybe even too transparent, but for whatever reason, not about this. It didn't make sense.

I began to wonder in earnest what Tess looked like, because now she was no longer just a character in a story that Mom and Dad had told me. Now she was someone who lived within an hour and a half away, with a family of her own, in an apartment, probably with a job, too, though I'd forgotten to ask Claire if she had one or what it was. She had a car with car seats.

"I'm sure that Claire is right," Mom said when I told her what Claire had said about Tess wanting to meet me. "We'll just have to wait and see what we can work out."

Dad had always told me that one day, when the time was right, I would be able to meet Tess, but after my conversation with Claire, and Mom acknowledging it as a step in the process of getting to that right time, it felt almost painful to wait another minute.

❖ Seven ❖

My Love, I wish we could run away together, the note began, written in swirly, round, and flirty handwriting on light blue rice paper. *Just you and me and Becky. I love you, Catherine.* I'd found the note folded several times into a small diamond shape nestled under the right corner of Dad's drawing board, where he kept notes and letters— not all from Catherine, but many of them.

Catherine was my father's lover. She and her husband, Anton, had moved to town with their young daughter, Lucy, earlier that summer before I started fifth grade, right around the same time that Mom and Dad decided to have an open marriage. Mom described the new marital arrangement to me as their decision to "branch out."

Initially, the arrangement involved spouse-swapping exclusively with Catherine and Anton. Things didn't work out with Anton and Mom, who later found another extramarital partner, but Catherine and Dad fell in love hard and maintained an intimate relationship for nearly a decade. I liked Catherine, who paid me a lot of attention, took me places, bought me clothes, and frequently told me that I was the most strikingly beautiful girl she'd ever seen. But I didn't know that she dreamed of running away with me and Dad until I found the note under Dad's drawing board, where I shouldn't have gone snooping around, much less read anything I found there, but I couldn't help myself.

I loved the smell of my parents' bedroom. It smelled like dark corners, brocade drapes, worn cotton, and pencil lead. Mom and Dad kept the heavy curtains drawn on the windows that faced the street, opening them for a few hours in the mid-morning to warm the room, then closing them in the afternoon. Mom's solid-oak antique dresser with brass drawer handles stood against the wall to the right of their bed, her side, with a small square mirror propped against the wall behind it, and baubles and rings and random buttons, sewing needles stuck into spools of thread, all laid out in disarray. It was a favorite place of mine to pause, as I was drawn early on to the collagist aspect of it, the art of its clutter and small yet vivid reflections of Mom. But Dad's desk held more appeal.

The quill dip pen and silver replacement nibs, ink jars and burnt sienna colored pencils, sketches of nudes, stacks of journals, foreign language guides and poetry books by Federico García Lorca. It was such a tender display—an elegant meditation on how thoughtful he was, how loving and deliberate. Standing in front of Dad's desk as a ten-year-old felt like worshipping at the altar of wisdom, art, and words, the nucleus of all that mattered in our household.

I refolded the note from Catherine and tucked it back under Dad's drawing board where I'd found it, feeling like both a loyal disciple and a devious traitor. Whether it was right or wrong that I'd found and read the note, it felt momentous, weirdly disquieting, and I knew that the one person I could tell about it who would keep a secret without judging me was Leah. I left Mom and Dad's room intent on telling Leah about it the next day at school.

✢ ✢

Leah and I were in separate fifth grade classes at Simonds Elementary School in Warner, so recess was our treasured time together. My teacher, Mrs. Gordon, was frumpy and stout with dull, wiry hair. Big-busted and broad-hipped, she wore bright red lipstick and favored green wool dresses and bulbous pearl earrings. It was late autumn, and when she chaperoned recess in the colder weather, she wore a fur-collared coat with a matching muff to keep her hands warm, and stood watch at the top of the steep knoll that dipped down into the playground.

Leah and I could see our breath as we ran up the hill to ask her how much more time there was left for recess. We'd been so wrapped up in our play that I'd forgotten to tell her about the note from Catherine, but I hoped there would still be time. Mrs. Gordon pulled one hand lazily out of her muff to check her wristwatch.

"You girls have got about fifteen minutes," she said, in her pinched-nose-sounding voice, and then stuffed her hand back inside her muff.

"OK, thanks!" Leah said, turning to me with a smile.

"You're a very pretty girl, Leah," Mrs. Gordon said, just as we were about to dash off. She *was* pretty, I thought, smiling at my best friend, as rosy red circles of blush spread across her cheekbones. "And you're very pretty, too, Becky," she continued, "for a black girl."

I wondered how she knew what most black girls even looked like. There wasn't a single other black girl in the school, or in town, for that matter.

"They're usually very ugly," continued Mrs. Gordon, scrunching up her face like she'd smelled something foul. "Very unattractive."

It felt like an invisible hand had grabbed my throat and started squeezing tighter and tighter in the quiet after Mrs. Gordon said "unattractive." She stood looking at the two of us, satisfied with the accuracy of her strident assessment. Leah and I turned to each other, and I thought maybe she could hear me choking as the invisible hand kept squeezing. Her eyes were glassy and bright with worry.

Until that moment, I had believed my parents and all their adult friends, Catherine, the grocery store clerks, the mailman, and all my teachers who had gone out of their way to tell me how special and beautiful I was. And if I was also black—about which there was still some question in terms of clear affirmation other than my own revelatory moment in writing when I was six— wouldn't it be within the realm of possibility for other black girls to be beautiful, too?

Then I remembered that time we had talked about slavery in the fourth grade the year before. The illustrations of black slave girls in the one book we'd read pictured them with giant, caricatured lips and tar-black skin and messed-up hair. Maybe Mrs. Gordon was right.

I thought about my dry skin that my brother ridiculed me about so relentlessly. My thick, coarse hair that I couldn't make move or sweep over my shoulders or do anything that *felt* pretty, so I'd pull a tight turtleneck shirt around my head and pretend it was long, glamourous hair, flipping my head back and forth to feel its weight and wonder. The times I'd tried to fit in with the blonde-headed daughters of my dad's best friend when they came to visit during the summers who were always dressed in neat, matching Garanimals outfits, colorful clips in their silky hair, while I always felt awkward, darker, and lesser when I looked at pictures of us posing together after they'd long gone.

The cognitive dissonance between what my parents and other

white adults had told me for the past ten years, and what Mrs. Gordon was now stating in such a self-satisfied, matter-of-fact manner, called up a sense of cruelty that I'd never experienced before. It was visceral, spiky, and gutting. Mrs. Gordon was my teacher, and teachers taught children factual information, like math and science and colors and how to spell. Parents only had to love us no matter what.

"Come on," Leah said, as if she could hear the gears turning inside my head. "Let's go play before recess is over." She grabbed my hand and clasped it tight as we ran back down the hill to play. We were different, though. The experience had changed us. It had changed *me*, and I felt my body shiver as a small cell of trauma began to metastasize.

✧ Eight ✧

"You have to choose!" Donna said, loud and bossy, arms crossed, standing outside in front of the school during recess one day. She was in my fifth grade class, and made friends by making them give up other ones. Leah and I mostly ignored her, so I wasn't terribly concerned when Donna confronted Leah seemingly out of nowhere, and gave her an ultimatum of choosing between me or her as a best friend. I assumed Leah would just blow her off.

It was the spring after Mrs. Gordon had made Leah pretty and me much less so, months after I'd found the note from Catherine, who continued to focus ever more intensely on me and all but ignored Leah and other kids when they were around. Our parents along with a few other couples in town had created a bacchanalia-like band of interchangeable friendships and loverships, and for a time, shared drop-off and pick-up duties, dinners, and weekend activities made it feel like all of us kids involved were everyone's kids. And like being in a blended family with stepparents and stepsiblings, we accepted it, if often begrudgingly, but each of us processed the experience differently. Leah didn't like it at all. She said it made her feel claustrophobic, like her world was closing in on her.

"I'll think about it," Leah said, and turned away from both me and Donna. I thought I must not have heard her correctly, and ran after her to catch up.

"Did you mean that?" I said, on the verge of tears.

"I don't know," she said. I knew Leah's facial expressions. Something was wrong; she was anxious. In that moment, the only thing that I could think might be making her so anxious was the thing that Mrs. Gordon had said to me, that we hadn't told our parents about or spoken of again after it happened. Maybe Leah had decided that I was damaged goods. It never occurred to me that the claustrophobia she had described feeling about the newly blurred lines and behaviors of our parents was beginning to overwhelm her.

"It's not that I don't like you anymore," Leah finally said, her voice shaky and unrecognizable. "I just need some space."

I began to cry.

"Don't cry, God," Leah said. "I'm just confused and I need some space. I'm sorry."

She turned to leave, and I watched her walk down the hill we'd run up and down hundreds of times, toward the jungle gym, where we'd hung on the bars until our hands burned and Donna now waited. I was absolutely devastated, blindsided. Leah was my *best* friend. How could this be happening? But children have inner lives before we know how to grow into them, and while I couldn't help but experience Leah's need for space as heartbreak and abandonment, Leah's own experience of it, I would learn much later, was entirely different.

I cried every day for a week, and then one afternoon, just after my eleventh birthday in May 1980, there was a development that temporarily took my mind off Leah and the abandonment by her I felt—an uncanny pivot to the primary source of underlying abandonment that I'd felt all throughout my childhood.

← →

"Kids! Come inside! We're going to have a family meeting!"

About six months after my visit with Claire, on a rare day when Sean and Riana and I were all home at the same time and, oddly, together outside, messing around and getting along, Dad cracked the screen door. The three of us looked at one another, bewildered. Dad had never called us "kids" before, and had certainly never called a family meeting.

"Somebody must have died," Sean said, and we all laughed, turning toward the house in one last wave of solidarity before things took an irrevocable turn. Mom was already seated at the table, composed and smiling. Dad ushered us in as if to a dinner party, and we sat to join Mom, looking back and forth at one another warily.

"We got a letter from Rebecca's biological mother, Tess," Dad announced. "And she's wondering if now would be a good time for her and Rebecca to meet. What does everybody think?"

I practically sprung up out of my chair. "Yes! I want to!" I clamored.

Less than a month later, Mom told me, without any discernible evidence of apprehension or concern, that Tess would come to our house on July 13, a few weeks away. Mom was excited, she said, and grateful that I had this opportunity to add "another dimension" to my life. Ever calm, steadily loving, she seemed to genuinely want this for me if I wanted this for me. And I did. I wanted to meet Tess, but more than anything, I wanted to see that she was real.

✦ Nine ✦

I stood in front of the bathroom mirror and fussed with my hair. A family friend who said she'd had some beauty salon experience before moving to Warner told me she could braid my hair like the actress Bo Derek from the movie *10*. But she'd only had time to do half of my head, so I pulled the braids back in colorful barrettes and wore the rest natural, but the natural didn't look natural to me. It looked too fluffy or frizzy, bunched up in places, uneven and stuck. I tried to separate single strands to tuck behind my ears, but each one sprung back in defiance, into the clutch of their thick collective clump.

I turned my attention to the outfit I'd chosen: a short-sleeve blouse with a blue-and-green print, a round neck, and neat buttons that I'd tucked into a pair of crisp white jeans. I had started to develop breasts, but wasn't yet wearing a bra, and suddenly felt self-conscious that the shape of my nipples might be visible under my blouse. I untucked my blouse and let it fall over the top of my jeans, trying to create more distance between the fabric and my bare chest.

Splotches of soapy watermarks that had splashed up from the tub onto the mirror started to appear bigger than they were, crowding the view of my reflection. I tilted my head to the side, in between the marks, trying to give a pose, Bonne Bell lip-glossed lips slightly open, my face the darker brown color it got from long summer days at the lake without sunscreen. I stared back at my reflection a few minutes longer, trying to reconcile who I saw with who I was, and what was about to happen. But what was about to happen was happening for the first time, and who I was was about to change forever.

Downstairs, I took a seat at the kitchen table along with Riana and Sean, who were seated across from each other, with Mom off to the left sitting in a chair next to Riana. Dad stood positioned toward the door, hands on his hips, one knee bent forward, shoulders straight—a gallant guardian of his carefully laid plans.

A large bouquet of fresh, seasonal wildflowers formed a centerpiece on the table. Maybe there was lemonade, pink from the frozen can. Or fresh cucumbers sliced with dark purple basil from the garden. The air was thick with who we were as a family—traces of hay and horse manure from the bottom of Riana's sneakers; the vague scent of pond water and fish entrails emanating from Sean's hands; pulses of Jean Naté after bath splash that Catherine had given me for my birthday; the gummy, sweet fragrance of Mom's watercolor palette; and the smell of damp leaves and dirt that had worn into Dad's dark blue sweatshirt from hours spent in the nearby swamp, looking for turtles.

My left arm was hitched over the back of my chair, upper body angled toward the door, when the same yellowish, beat-up Chevy Nova with the car seats in the back that Roy and Claire had driven to visit pulled into the driveway. I jumped out of my seat; the rest of my family stayed where they were, except for Dad, who walked toward the door behind me and said, "Rebecca Anne Carroll, this is your life!" I barely even acknowledged his lighthearted effort at lifting some of the tension in the room by echoing a line from a famous TV show that predated me by twenty years. With my eyes locked on the driveway, I watched as the driver and passenger doors of the car opened simultaneously like the hatches of a spaceship, and Roy and Tess emerged from either side.

They walked together across the driveway and toward the door in what felt like slow motion. Tess stepped onto the porch first, and I opened the door to welcome her inside. With the door still ajar, Roy's hand holding it just above us, Tess and I sank into each other's skin. She smelled like sandalwood and peaches, and her body felt liquid as we embraced, not just fluid but vast, like a wide body of water in which I should have felt like I was drowning, but instead felt like I'd suddenly developed gills.

"I have to sit down for this." Those are the first words I can remember hearing Tess say. She may have said "hi" or "hello" before we hugged, but I only registered the physical sensation of her arms around me before hearing her voice, which sounded cool and distant, incongruous with what I was feeling, a visceral familiarity. She had shoulder-length, beach-wavy brown hair and hazel eyes, and I could hardly believe how stunning she was. I searched hard for flickers of our resemblance, but found nothing.

Tess settled into a chair at the table, while I stood next to her, hands at my side, like a servant ready to deliver myself in whatever form she might order. Roy stood, too, and when our eyes met briefly, his expression was softer than I'd seen before, vulnerable almost. It was the first time in the eleven years I'd known him that he remained quiet in a roomful of people. He hovered protectively over me and Tess at a safe distance while we tried to intuit how to move around each other. I didn't know what to say. I'd never not known what to say.

"Maybe you two want to go for a walk into town?" Mom suggested, breaking the silence.

I looked at Tess for her answer, and she nodded, "Yes, that's probably a good idea."

Dad and Roy fell into their familiar conversational pace behind us as Tess and I walked out of the house and headed toward town. Tess carried her sandals in her hand and walked barefoot on the shoulder of the highway, wearing a pale green cotton wraparound skirt she'd dyed herself—she loved to dye her own clothes, she told me—and a casual, ribbed tank top that showed off her smooth, sun-kissed shoulders.

I felt overdressed in my blouse and jeans, and too hot as the July sun blazed down on our backs. We walked the near mile into the center of town, with me mostly silent and Tess talking about dyeing her clothes, what colors she gravitated toward (neutrals), and how essential cotton was as a basic summer item. Her mood was more relaxed than it had been back at the house, if not entirely warm, less distant, almost chatty. She mentioned her love of sewing and quilting, both passions passed down from her mother, Lena, whom she called by name but didn't say much else about.

We walked past the small stretch of road before town, after Dr. Levis's office, where there were no houses, just overgrown briar patches and hilly, vacant sandlots that some of the kids from town used as a track for riding their ATVs. Suddenly Warner seemed dismal and limited as I walked alongside this woman, my birth mother, who appeared so effortlessly polished, so organically nonchalant, and from a place where, I was absolutely certain, kids didn't get drunk and drive their ATVs around and around in circles for sport.

At the Variety Store and Restaurant, we sat on bar stools and ordered milkshakes, while I tried to find the nerve to say something. I felt distinctly not myself, the self I'd known for eleven years—never without words. Tess was not quite a stranger, but neither was she an acquaintance, or immediately familiar. I stared over the counter, through the open service window of the prep kitchen where food was ordered and placed, and a large fan faced outward, whirring like a windmill.

"You don't have any questions for me? I thought a daughter of mine would have more questions," Tess said, reverting to the distant tone she had back at the house after we'd first hugged.

"I do, I mean . . ."

Salt and pepper shakers sat in twos spread evenly apart along the counter, like couples at a wedding altar, the tall silver napkin dispensers as wedding officiants. I hadn't taken more than one sip of my milkshake when I blurted out what I thought was a logical question, and one that I realized only after I said it that I wanted an answer to: "What was my father like?"

"Basically, he was a dog," Tess answered, without a moment's pause. I'd never heard a man described as a dog before, and I wondered what it meant. "He was a jive-ass black man who could bullshit like nobody's business."

I felt chastened for asking such an unwelcome question, and resolved not to ask anything else for fear this moment together would disappear as quickly as it had materialized. Tess asked me about school, and what my interests were. I tried to give the right answers after failing to ask the right question. She seemed mildly unimpressed as I told her about ballet, that my teacher was black. "Oh," Tess said. "A token, like you." I didn't know what she meant—the only tokens I knew about were in the set of green, yellow, blue, and red wood tokens used as game pieces for our Parcheesi board game.

Tess paid for our milkshakes, and we walked back home, again with Tess taking the lead talking about her baby boys, how poopy and smelly their diapers were sometimes, and her best friends,

Joy and Nancy, who also each had baby boys. But I only heard frag-
ments of what she was saying because I was trying to think of how
to be better for her. I was not prepared for how unlovable I felt
in her company. I did not anticipate how shocking the bone-deep
ache of wanting her approval would feel.

Back at the house, I disappeared upstairs to my room to quickly
make her a card out of drawing paper and markers. In it, I wrote,
cheerfully, an appeal of sorts: *I love you always!* I also brought my
autograph book, where I collected signatures and notes from
friends and family members, and asked her to sign it. After reading my card, she wrote: *Love always, too. Tess.*

I was too overcome by the experience to be able to articulate
or even fully understand the swirl of emotions raging within me,
but I knew one thing: I needed to see Tess again. As soon as she
and Roy pulled out of the driveway to head back home, I asked
Mom and Dad when that could happen. A month later, Dad and
Catherine drove me to Portsmouth and dropped me off at Tess's
apartment for a weekend visit with her and her family.

Ten

W*e pulled into a paved parking* lot with two brown clapboard tenement houses on opposite ends. A few beat-up cars with broken windows and rusty fenders lined the lot, and a lone motorcycle leaned on a short kickstand, threatening to fall over. It was drizzling, and the air was wet and damp; when Dad and I got out of the car, a mangy-looking cat darted underneath the one parked next to ours. Catherine stayed behind—Dad told her he wouldn't be long. Two plastic Big Wheel bikes, a doll with her arm missing, and a couple of empty soda cans littered the front lawn as we walked up the path to Tess's front door.

We were greeted by a handsome man with a full head of dark black curls and beautiful, beaming eyes. "Welcome," he said. "I'm Miguel, welcome, welcome!" Miguel had a just barely noticeable accent, and I remembered that Tess had told me during our walk back to the house after milkshakes that her partner was Puerto Rican.

"I can't stay," Dad said, shaking Miguel's hand. "But thank you for having Becky for a visit."

"Of course!" Miguel said with a smile. "Tess's upstairs. Come in, Becky."

I was carrying a little bamboo suitcase that Catherine had given me, round with a wooden latch key.

"OK, bye, little one," Dad said, and gave me a squeeze at the doorstep.

"Bye, Dave," I said.

Dad jogged back to the car, where Catherine sat waiting, and I watched as they pulled out of the lot.

Tess and Miguel's two-bedroom apartment was cozy, with a modest-sized living room, where there were pretty cotton curtains, a well-worn couch with patchwork quilts that Tess had sewn, hanging plants, a TV, and a midsize stereo system, with records by Phoebe Snow and Earl Klugh stacked below. Throw pillows on the carpeted floor against the wall served as both seats and safe play space for the boys, and a spindle-back wooden chair sat near a door to the back, where a clothing line stretched across the yard to the apartment units on the other side.

"Hello, Rebecca," Tess said, midway down the staircase between the front door and the living room. She smiled, but didn't hug me. Instead, I hugged her, but let go quickly after feeling her body tense up in my arms. "The babies are sleeping," she said. "But they'll be up soon and then you can meet your brothers."

I loved them instantly. Mateo had his father's jet black hair and warm brown skin, and an undeniable raw magnetism. Sebastian had Tess's skin tone, unusually long eyelashes, fat baby cheeks, and wisps of brown curls. I held and changed them, played with them, rocked and read to them, and made them laugh all day on the first day of my visit. These were the children my birth mother had kept, and in their company, I felt kept, too.

That night, Tess and I left the boys with Miguel to go see a movie called *The Rose*, starring a very young Bette Midler, at the Portsmouth Music Hall, an old Victorian theater in the center of town. It was packed, and in the hot, muggy August heat, the room smelled like sweat and cigarettes and stale buttered popcorn. We

went with a couple of Tess's girlfriends, and the crowd was raucous, a range of merry, austere, and fervent faces all around us. It
was exhilarating to be surrounded by such an animated audience
of adults, each a wild and captivating character to watch, even
before the movie started.

I loved the movie, entranced by Midler's lead performance as
a feverishly talented and troubled rock star in the '60s, so full of
ache and grit and sorrow.

The next night, Tess decided we should go dancing at a disco
called the Uptown, which didn't open until after midnight. We
arrived at about 1:30 a.m. At eleven years old, I was thrilled to be
staying up so late, although it also felt a little like a test. As if Tess
was giving me another opportunity to prove myself as the daughter she hoped I would be. Dancing was something I was good at,
so I felt confident and excited.

Young people, mostly in their twenties it appeared, also
mostly white, gathered at the entrance behind velvet ropes in
bell-bottom jeans, platform shoes, long silk scarves, and tight T-
shirts. I had borrowed one of Tess's elastic-waisted skirts to wear
as a strapless dress, which made me look older than my eleven
years. I loved how it flowed when I twirled around. Once we
were inside, strobes threw hatchets of light across the dark, shad-
owy dance floor, while bodies shimmied and bumped up against
one another.

Tess and I danced in a group with her friends, but when "Celebration" by Kool & the Gang came on, I got lost in my own
world. *American Bandstand* was one of my favorite shows, and I had
just watched Kool & the Gang perform this song as guests. I both
saw and didn't see these agile black men singing and moving in
stylistic relays on *American Bandstand*—caught somewhere in between internalizing the raceless indoctrination by my parents and

untangling the visceral pull toward blackness, as I'd felt with Easy Reader, Mrs. Rowland, and Anita.

Soon, without my even realizing it, a circle of people had gathered around me on the dance floor, clapping and cheering me on, impressed by this little brown girl bold enough to steal the spotlight at a disco club full of people twice, even three times her age.

When I realized what was happening, I looked to find Tess in the crowd. Her face flickered in and out, and I saw her signal for me to come back to where we'd been dancing with the rest of the group. And then we left, abruptly. Our drive home began quiet, and I looked out the window at quiet buildings and houses illuminated by the soft glow of sunrise.

"Listen," she finally said. "Just because people in Warner have objectified you as this precious, exotic child doesn't mean you're anything special here." Her response to my dancing and the attention it garnered, the tone of her voice, was so captious that I instinctively looked down at my dress to make sure my boobs hadn't accidently popped out. Again, I felt chastised, just as I had when I'd asked about my birth father the day we met.

"It's a disservice to you, too, because your packaging misrepresents your substance," Tess said, stringing together words I'd never heard before. "Do you know what that means? It means people think you're something special just because you look different. Because you can be charming and are maybe a little precocious," she explained, using another word I'd never heard before.

"Oh," I said, quietly, feeling overwhelmed with sorrow.

"If you keep believing all these adults who are constantly telling you how special and exotic you are, you're going to end up cultivating a sense of entitlement, which is a super unattractive quality," Tess said.

"I'm sorry." That's all I could think to say. I felt like Tess was shaming me for believing my parents, the people she had entrusted to raise me, a decision it seemed almost immediately clear after we met she regretted having made.

It was almost three a.m. by the time we went to bed, so I slept for much of the morning. When I got up, I played with the boys, whose skin smelled so good, and who giggled with such delight, that I forgot about what Tess had said to me about my packaging and my substance, and those other words like "exotic" and "precocious" and "entitlement." We went fabric shopping at the mall, where Tess said I could pick out whatever material I wanted, and she would sew me a sundress with a matching cloth purse. I chose a modern design with blues and grays and pink flowers.

We went back to Uptown again that night. This time I knew not to draw too much attention to myself, and decided to sit out the first few songs at the bar, where Roy worked as a bartender. He hastily served me a ginger ale and then disappeared at the other end to serve real drinkers, who were shouting out their orders, trying to be heard over the din of disco music from the dance floor.

It would have been uncharacteristic of Roy to pay special attention to me, even though I was visibly anxious and looked out of place. I wore a tank top and a long striped skirt, this one my own, and sat at the far end of the bar against the wall, opposite the dance floor. I was trying to be as innocuous as possible, while still pulling off enough maturity so that I didn't appear to be the child I was. Two sips into my ginger ale, a white man probably in his late thirties sat down on the stool next to me, and asked if he could buy me a drink. He had greasy brown hair and ruddy skin. His eyes looked like Jell-O balls through the tint of his '70s eyeglasses, wiggly and gelatinous, and his upper lip curled when he spoke.

I told him no thanks, that I already had a drink and was fine, trying to maintain my composure, trying to call up role models for such circumstances but unable to think of any. He inched closer, and I could feel his breath on me. "I bet you're a real spitfire in bed," he whispered, his words snaking into my ears.

All I could think to do was look away from him, but he kept at it. "You playing hard to get, huh?"

I jumped off my stool and ran out onto the dance floor to find Tess.

"He was just trying to pick you up, you're overreacting," Tess said on the way home, disparagingly, her hands gripped tight on the wheel. I started to cry, which annoyed her even more. I'd wanted to cry the night before, when I'd attracted too much attention on the dance floor, but had managed to keep it together by just staying quiet. But now she was angry at me for being hit on by a guy at a club that *she* had taken me to—a fact she didn't mind using to push her own point further.

"What did you expect? You were sitting at a bar." She never faltered when she spoke, or lost her cool, as if it were totally normal to take an eleven-year-old to a club and let her sit alone at a bar. Would she have let any eleven-year-old sit at a bar? What if it had been Sebastian or Mateo in ten years? Or the daughter of a friend? Or a girl she'd never met, but who was just sitting there by herself? I couldn't understand if she was more upset because her eleven-year-old daughter didn't know how to handle the advances of a creepy older guy, or if she just expected eleven-year-olds in general to have a better grasp on such things.

When we got home, though, she softened some, and we stayed up talking. She gave me a lecture about how most men are ultimately scared of women like her, like the woman I would grow up to become, strong and opinionated.

Bancroft women, she said, had a history of bringing men to their knees. "Don't be passive," Tess told me, sitting at the end of the couch, shoes off, bare toes curled up under her legs. "You were passive back there at the bar, and that's not who Bancroft women are."

That's when it started. When I felt my breath slowing and my muscles loosening, when I first felt her words begin to replace mine, the sound of her voice rising up under my own. Her cadence was so confident, her points so precise. I felt hooked up to her, as if her language, her thoughts and explanations, were all coursing through my veins like a blood transfusion.

"One time, when I was hitching across the country with a girl-friend," Tess said as the sun began to rise through the window behind us, "I was just a few years older than you, and we stopped at a gas station to pee. This big machismo guy started talking shit to us. And I just said to him, 'You wanna fuck right now? Let's go.'" She laughed, shaking her head out of pity. "He got right back in his truck and drove off. Men can't handle strong, assertive women. They just, like, can't."

This idea of women having power over men was a first for me. In Warner, we all lived within the narrative that Dad had written for us—where we lived, how we interacted with one another, what we should believe about the world outside our home, and the blurred boundaries we should accept inside our home. The open marriage, Mom had told me, was Dad's idea, but she trusted him, she said, his creative genius and his vision for a beautiful life.

Tess and I slept only a few hours that morning before the boys woke up, and then soon it was time for Tess to drive me home. She had a different car now, a blue Chevy Chevette, and we buckled in, just the two of us, for the drive to Warner. Tess had decided at the last minute that she wanted to take this opportunity to introduce me to her grandmother Frances, my great-grandmother by birth, whose house in New Durham was on the way, the same house where Tess had lived when she was pregnant with me, and where I spent the first three weeks of my life. Frances, Tess said as we drove, had grown extremely attached to me during those three weeks, when she took over responsibility for my care. She would be happy to see me.

The house was dark inside, and slightly eerie. Frances was sitting in a rocking chair near a window in the living room. She was quite old but still somewhat lucid. I recall her wearing glasses, a housedress and slippers, with weathered skin, gray hair, and a wide girth that filled out the seat of her chair. She smiled and held out her hand to me when Tess introduced us. Frances didn't say anything, but she held onto my hand for an extra few minutes, slowly smoothing her thumb over the tops of my knuckles.

We didn't stay long, and after Tess delivered me safely back home in Warner, we said our goodbyes and promised to write. Tess wished me luck with middle school, which I'd be starting in a couple of weeks, and said she would work on my dress when she had time, and send it as soon as she could. The dress came as a package in the mail a week later. A straight, calf-length shift with thin shoulder straps in the material I'd picked out from the fabric store, along with a little matching satchel stitched to perfection, and maybe even lovingly.

✦ Eleven ✦

We'd always lived hand to mouth on Dad's meager teaching income and the occasional sale of one of Mom's paintings, but I'd never felt poor before I started middle school. On the first day of sixth grade, in my blue Sassoon baggies and the brown lace-up shoes from TJ Maxx that Catherine had bought for me, because my parents couldn't afford new school clothes, I immediately realized that middle school was going to be about name brands and money—who had it and who didn't. Nike sneakers, Northern Isles sweaters, white turtlenecks with little red hearts, L.L.Bean canvas backpacks, and colorful Trapper Keepers were everywhere.

Kids arrived in Jeep Wagoneers, Volkswagens, and Volvos, dropped off by their parents. They didn't take the same yellow school bus that I took the fifteen miles from Warner to New London, where Kearsarge Regional Middle School was located. The middle school served a district of seven neighboring towns. As in elementary school, I was the only black student at Kearsarge.

The girls, all pretty with shiny hair and perfect skin, traveled in cliques, small groups of palpable power, and the boys watched them. One clique stood out in the lunchroom, where the social caste system of a school is always laid the barest. Nicole, from ballet, who had since moved from Warner to New London, was part of this group, but the clear leader was Ella, who looked to me exactly like Brooke Shields from *The Blue Lagoon*, which I'd seen with Catherine over the summer. Her long brown hair pulled back into a neat ponytail, its smooth, slick strands brushing her shoulder blades when she turned to talk to the girl sitting next to her. She had varnish-brown eyes, a perfectly proportioned nose, and unblemished, glowing skin.

Standing in the line for hot lunch, I could almost hear the confidence in Ella's voice, the cadence of her laughter, the pitch of her privilege, as she and her friends opened their brown bags of carefully packed sandwiches and carrot sticks and cookies. Popular girls never ate hot lunch. It was completely stigmatized. If you ate hot lunch, which was served up on orange marbled-plastic trays with small compartments for a meat, a vegetable, a starch, and a dessert, you were immediately labeled a second-class citizen—someone who ate disgusting processed food, whose parents couldn't afford to buy healthy groceries.

I was determined on that first day of middle school to become part of the popular clique. I wanted what Ella had, what she embodied. I watched as the boys looked at her and then laughed among themselves, holding the same power. One boy, who looked like Ella's twin, in kelly green chinos and a pale yellow Izod shirt, walked over to her table and said a few words, grinned inside the frame of his straight, preppy haircut, and then returned to his own table. This, I soon learned, was Nate, Ella's boyfriend, who sat at the corollary popular boys' table with his best friend, Ryan, an achingly beautiful boy with greenish eyes and flecks of white in his eyelashes and hair.

I introduced myself to Ella, who was either amused or impressed by my verve, standing in front of her holding my hot lunch tray, and gestured for me to sit in the empty seat of a girl who was absent that day. It was a temporary arrangement, and even though I felt like she and the other girls liked me, including Nicole, whom I already knew, the next day I was relegated to a second-tier, adjacent table with Tammy from ballet. I worked hard to gain Ella's attention and approval, and morphed almost overnight into a brown-skinned imitation of her—forcing my hair back into a ponytail, begging Catherine to buy me Izod shirts and Nike sneakers and white shoelaces with red hearts.

After that first day in the lunchroom, Ella and I were friendly in the classes we had together, and waved to each other in between the classes we didn't. "Hey, Becky!" she'd yell, from inside the circle of friends she was always surrounded by. "Hey, Ella!" I'd shout back, enthusiastically.

In the second month of school, Ella invited me to her house for a sleepover. Her home was neat and spacious with a long staircase where three large black-and-white framed photographs lined the wall. The photos were close-ups of young black children, some wearing school uniforms or printed smocks, all with braided hair and glistening faces, round ebony cheeks and skinny limbs. In one of the photographs, a little girl in just a white tank top and underwear sat in a chair outside, facing the camera with a wide grin, while getting blood drawn from her arm.

"Those are pictures from Kenya," Ella explained when she saw me looking at them. "We lived there for a year so my dad could help them. Children in Africa need a lot of help because lots of them don't have hospitals."

That night, Ella had planned for Ryan and Nate to come over to play pool with us in her basement rec room. *It couldn't possibly be this easy to suddenly be friends with the popular kids*, I thought. "Yeah, it's just Becky Carroll and Ella here, Ann," I overheard Ella's mother tell Ryan's mom, Ann, on the phone in the kitchen. "Becky

Carroll, from Warner." Ella and I were finishing up our pizza at the raised island in the center of the kitchen.

"Oh, OK. Sure. Next time then, OK, bye." Ella's mom hung up and, with an oh-well shrug, told us that Ryan couldn't come because his mom said he had homework to do, even though it was a Friday night. I was devastated. Why had they made a plan and then changed it so suddenly? And what about Nate? Was he still coming? He was not, but nobody said why. Did this have to do with me? Would Ryan have canceled if it were Nicole who was staying over? Or another white friend of Ella's? Did Nate and Ryan decide, or did their parents decide, that Ella was just being nice to me, but that I could never earn or live up to their social status? Ella's mom made us popcorn while we watched TV, and after that, we went to bed.

Back at school on Monday, I couldn't face the fact that Ryan and Nate had canceled on us, and instead lied to a few friends and told them that Ryan and Nate had come over, and we played pool and it had all been super fun and great. Word spread quickly, and when Ella found out that I'd lied, she approached me in the hallway when she saw me walking back to class after using the bathroom, while she was on her way to the library.

"I'm not mad, Becky," Ella said, charitably. "We just want to help you."

Like the people in Kenya, I thought.

Ella forgave me, so everyone else did, too. The next day, she even bumped another girl from the top-tier popular girls' table in the lunchroom so that I could sit there now. Popularity worked in strange and arbitrary ways, and I wasn't about to question it.

Nate and I had math class together, and knowing that I would never pose a threat to Ella as girlfriend material—she was the prettiest and most popular girl in school; how could I possibly compete with that?——I positioned myself in service to Nate, and became his friend and confidante. We talked on the phone almost every night. The call to New London was then a toll call, billed by the minute if the number was out of a certain radius. Somehow, even though I was the one between us without any money, I was always the one who called Nate, whose father was a teacher at our regional high school, as well as a member of the New London Country Club. My phone bills are the stuff of my family lore, and we had our phone shut off more than once because of them.

Ryan, though, who held out for weeks before forgiving me about the lie after Ella's sleepover, was the boy I longed for. We were often playful with each other, but he didn't like me "that way," Nate told me. None of the boys did. I accepted this, but didn't give up hope. Or perhaps I knew it, but didn't believe it.

There was something about Ryan that seemed different from the other boys. He was quietly charismatic, a gentle thinker with a placid demeanor. I thought that if any of the popular boys would ever be able to actually see me, it would be Ryan.

✦ Twelve ✦

I had just brushed my teeth to get ready for bed when Riana stormed up the stairs and shoved past me through the bathroom, into our bedroom on the other side. I could feel the rage ricochet off her body before she slammed the door so hard behind her that Mom's big jar of Noxzema and our toothbrush cup both tumbled off the shelf above the sink and fell onto the floor, cracking the jar's cover. I'd never seen Riana drenched in fury, radiating raw pain, and it was terrifying.

"Are you OK?" I said quietly through the door.

"Shut up! Go away!!" Riana shouted back. I could hear the tears catching her words, and the fight in her voice.

I went downstairs and sat at the kitchen table with Mom, who said, herself on the verge of tears, that there'd been an accident, and someone had hurt Riana.

"Who?" I asked.

"We don't know yet, Beck. Let's just give Riana the space she needs right now."

My sister and I had become less close since I'd started middle school and insisted on being popular, something Riana didn't care about, but we still shared a room and some secrets, talked together like sisters. I wanted to go and try to talk with her again, to make sure she was OK, but the sound of her anger when she'd shouted "Go away!" kept me downstairs with Mom, who made us hot chocolate that we drank in silence.

About an hour later, I went back upstairs and pressed my ear to the door, before tiptoeing into our room and slipping quietly into my bed. I stared at the ceiling while Riana finally slept. Nobody talked about that night, after which Riana shut down completely. But I was too distracted to be worried about what was going on with my sister, as she became distant and moody. I was focused almost obsessively on my new relationship with Tess and our next visit: a day trip to Boston.

The city of Boston was a big deal if you lived in rural New Hampshire. It was the closest major city, and had tall buildings and museums and fancy restaurants. It's also where Tess's mother, Lena, lived and worked as a cab driver, and Tess wanted me to meet her, just as she had wanted me to meet Frances. It wasn't immediately clear whether Tess thought it was more important for me to meet these women in her and my matrilineal succession, or for these women to see me as proof of concept that Tess had given birth to a daughter.

Tess's love and admiration for Frances was certain, but her loss of Lena, when she spoke her name aloud, was palpable.

"She was so self-aware, and always commanded the attention of everyone in the room," Tess said as we crossed the park inside the Boston Common, Sebastian squawking from his stroller, a little wheeled chariot, as dozens of gray squirrels darted across the path in front of us. I'd never seen so many gray squirrels before. "And Lena's love for her children, us, it knew no bounds."

About halfway through the park, Tess paused. "This is where I met your father," she said. "He was playing guitar right there on the grass, serenading any woman foolish enough to stop and listen."

Since the disastrous response to my asking about him the day Tess and I had first reunited just a few months before, I hadn't brought him up again, and when she gave me this small piece of unprompted insight, I decided not to push it further. Instead, I just nodded and smiled. We continued walking, headed toward a nearby McDonald's, where Tess had arranged for us to meet Lena, who had taken Mateo out for a birthday lunch. Tess, Sebastian, and I were coming to pick him up.

The park had been fairly empty of people until we came upon a couple of black men walking toward us in the other direction. "Hey, little mama," one of them said to me, his man chest puffed up under his dark leather jacket. "How you doin', brown sugar," the other echoed, cranking his neck as we passed. "Mmmmm-hmmmmm, whew, mama! You look *good!*" Their overtures were frightening to me. These black men weren't at all like Easy Reader, who was so graceful, gentle, and good-natured. Instead, these men in the park seemed erratic and slick, and made me think of a different black male TV character.

Huggy Bear was the loose-lipped street hustler on *Starsky & Hutch*, a show that I watched religiously because I had an enormous crush on David Soul, the blond, blue-eyed actor who played Hutch. Huggy was always ogling and objectifying women on the show, staring at their behinds when they bent over, trying to charm them into bed. It was never completely clear whether he was an actual pimp—which I wouldn't have known anything about anyway—but he was always dressed in a leather jacket, with a wide-collared shirt unbuttoned to mid-chest, or no shirt at all, a large-brimmed hat, and a scarf tied around his neck.

These men were looking at me the same way that Huggy looked at the women on *Starsky & Hutch*. We could still hear them when we reached the other side of the park and stepped out onto the sidewalk. Tess hadn't flinched, and when I turned to her, clearly rattled, she looked at me, exasperated. It seemed there was no end to the ways in which I could disappoint her. "They're just jive, bored black men, don't pay them any mind. They're tired is what they are."

Beyond her exasperation, though, I had also started to notice that Tess often seemed to be trying to emulate the way certain black people sounded, like Nell from the TV show *Gimme a Break!* She'd say things like "Girl, please" or "Listen, sugar britches." It was mostly her inflection, but this was just my third visit with her, and I felt stupid even trying to read her voice, much less her emotions.

When we arrived at the McDonald's, Lena and Mateo were already there, sitting at a booth in the back. Lena was smoking a cigarette; a paper cup of coffee that looked like it might be cold sat on the table in front of her. Mateo ran into my arms, and Tess picked up Sebastian out of the stroller and held him on her hip. The four of us stood in front of Lena, waiting for someone to speak.

"Lena, this is Rebecca." Tess introduced me to her mother with the certainty of a court prosecutor presenting incontestable evidence. Lena looked at me with vacant eyes. She wore her long, leaden hair in a low bun, and her shoulders were hunched under an oversized khaki-colored jacket.

"Hi," I said tentatively. She nodded at me, took a drag of her cigarette, and looked away. Lena seemed almost ghostlike, as if I could see the smoke from her cigarette sucked down into her throat, cloudy and ashen, making lazy loops inside her lungs. There was a dire stillness about her, nothing like the vibrant woman Tess had described, who hosted literary salons at their home in Boston, and loved men and language and music.

"Thanks for being so generous with Mateo, Lena," Tess said.

Lena nodded.

"Mateo, thank Lena for such a generous gesture." Tess looked at her oldest boy, who I was now holding on my hip. "Go ahead, don't be rude," she insisted.

"Thank you, Lena," Mateo, just barely two years old, said dutifully. I gave him a squeeze, and whispered in his ear, "Good job."

After a few minutes, we turned to leave, the smell of french fry grease thicker with every step toward the door. I looked back at Lena, sitting under a broken fluorescent light, fading into the darkness as if I'd never seen her at all.

Thirteen

I hadn't heard her voice in what felt like forever.

"Hey," Leah said, suddenly standing next to me at my locker in school the morning after my Boston trip with Tess.

"Hey!" I said, maybe a little too eagerly. I had no idea what had prompted her to suddenly start talking to me again, and I truly did not care. Our bond could withstand anything. I felt it in my bones.

"I miss you," she said somberly. "And I'm so sorry. I don't know what happened, but I felt confused, and things were so weird with our parents, and I want us to be friends again."

"Oh my God! I miss you SO much!" I nearly shrieked, throwing my arms around her. She hugged me back, and before she could say anything else, I started to tell her in breathless, rapid spitfire about everything that had happened in the months we'd been apart. "I met Tess! She's so pretty! And I have brothers, they're so cute! And we went to Boston!"

"OK! Slow down!" Leah laughed, her smile like a precious family heirloom temporarily lost and then miraculously found.

"Want to sit with me at the popular table? I'm sitting with Ella and those guys at the popular table. Isn't that cool?"

"I know, I saw! That's great!" Leah, whom I'd seen sitting in the lunchroom with friends from elementary school when we'd first started sixth grade, seemed happier for me and my social mobility than she was interested in getting her own seat at the popular table. Ella granted my request to give Leah a seat, which meant bumping another girl permanently. Leah was happy to sit with us, and I was happy to have her back as my best friend.

Toward the end of sixth grade, a break-dancing crew came to perform at our school. Leah and I sat together on the gym bleachers along with our new friends, the popular kids, Ryan among them. Ryan had a quirky, grown-sounding voice, and made observations about the world around him with an unfussy sense of wonder. There was an elasticity to the way he spoke, an inviting pause in between sentences, that stretched further with every additional word. "Sit here, Becky Carroll," Ryan had said, tapping the space on the bleachers next to him when Leah and I had first walked in. He liked to say my whole name.

When a small crew of all black boys came out to give a high-energy performance, I found myself feeling torn between a sense of giddiness and the fear of being found out—that if I expressed any of the excitement I felt at seeing this group of black boys perform, I would be exposing *myself* as black. Their show was so electric, though, and by the time it was over, my cheeks hurt from smiling. The boys stuck around afterward to answer whatever questions we might have, or for the congratulatory attention they hoped we'd lavish upon them, and which they were probably used to with other less-white audiences.

Most of the students dispersed, while a few of us lingered to avoid going back to class. Nobody said anything about the show or the black boys who were standing so nearby. It was as if they didn't even exist. I casually looked over my shoulder to see one of the boys holding his glance toward me. Youthful and serious, round-shouldered and alluring, he bit his lip when he caught my eye and smiled a sweet, mischievous grin that gave me butterflies. I smiled back, flirtatiously.

Over the sound of sneaker squeaks on the gym floor and the cacophony of adolescent chatter, I heard Ryan say, pointed yet dispassionately, "Looks like somebody has a crush." I snapped out of what felt like a mini-trance, as if I'd been caught in some sort of shameful act.

"What?" I said, trying to come off as casually disinterested as possible. "Are you kidding? No way." I pushed my whole body into Ryan, coltishly, shaking my head and laughing, mindfully signaling to him that I would never be interested in a black boy.

I innately understood that an open display of solidarity with blackness would make me less viable, less valuable, as a member of the popular clique. I couldn't gamble with the popularity I'd effectively banked for the sake of this black boy, who was only going to return to whatever faraway city where black people lived, never to be seen again. Ryan pushed back, and we all left the gym in a highly engineered herd of homogeneity.

I turned back one last time to see the boy I'd betrayed. He shook his head, his face conveying what he'd known all along, that I was a sellout. And then Leah caught my eye. I could tell that she'd seen the whole exchange, and looked at me now so tenderly, with an expression so full of empathy, as if I'd missed an opportunity she knew I needed to have, that I almost turned back and run after the boy with the mischievous grin before he disappeared for good.

✣ Fourteen ✣

I didn't have my hair brushed out entirely until I was twelve years old. For years when I was younger, I'd let Dad use a soft-bristle brush to gently fluff it into a perfectly round afro, but after a while I stopped letting him, and my parents just started to kind of ignore it. Tess said I should have a black person do something with my hair, and during my next visit with her after our trip to Boston, she brought me to Ida's Beauty Shop, the oldest black-owned hair salon in Portsmouth, where there was a small but vibrant black population.

The shop was on a back road on the way out of town in a modest-sized converted ranch-style home, with one bathroom and a row of three hair dryers against the wall to the left of the main chair. Ida yanked at my hair with a metal pick until she could pull it all the way through from top to end, shaking her head at the state of my hair. It was completely snarled and matted in the back from years of neglect, and every tug felt like a kind of punishment Ida didn't want to enact, though she knew it was for my own good.

Tess sat on a black faux leather couch in the waiting area and flipped through an old *Ebony* magazine as I sat in the salon chair facing a mirror above a shelf with hot combs, hairpins, and large jars of Vaseline. Ida, tall and regal, with her own hair straightened and permed, stood over me, doing the Lord's work on a Friday afternoon, stopping every now again to say something like, "Whoever? *What* in the name? My goodness, chile!" Ida, whose clear eyes reflected the burden of history and the patience it required, was also an ordained minister, Tess told me after.

Once Ida could work a pick through my hair, she took a hot comb to it. I could feel the heat on my neck as she slid the comb through my suddenly long and luxurious hair, like a hot knife through butter. I had no idea it was even possible for my hair to be straightened like this, but once it was almost as smooth and silky as that of the white girls at school, I never wanted to wear it any other way.

"You can't get it wet, chile," Ida said. "It'll go right on back to what it was if you get it wet." I nodded my head dutifully. "And find someone who can help you keep up with it, all right now?" I refrained from telling her that there was no someone who could help me keep up with my hair. In the moment, though, I was too caught up in my new straight-haired glory, so I just kept nodding. "You need to wrap it at night, keep it greased at the scalp. You don't have to wash it but once a week. Use a deep conditioner. Get some shea butter. You got a bonnet you can wear to bed?" Ida's voice trailed behind us as we left the shop.

I didn't care if I never showered or washed my hair again so long as it stayed just like this. That night I babysat for friends of Tess, and I remember standing in front of a mirror in their living room after the kids had gone to bed, flipping this new long, straight hair from side to side, the way I'd always wanted to, the way I used to pretend with a turtleneck shirt over my head when I was younger.

But then it rained, and just like Ida had told me, my hair went back to what it was—frizzy and coarse, all its luster gone, curls shrunk up around my ears. It was at least long enough that its own weight forced it to fall downward rather than sticking upward, like it had when it was an afro, an untamable mess.

✢ Fifteen ✢

Slave Day was a time-honored, annual tradition at Kearsarge Regional Middle School.

The way it worked was that seventh grade boys would bid on the seventh grade girls, and vice versa, and the highest bidder would then buy that girl or boy and make them their personal slave for the day. The ramifications of this for me, the only black girl in the school, occurred to no one—not my parents, not my friends' parents, not teachers or the principal. Not a single white adult took issue with the fact that in 1981 rural New Hampshire, a black child, me, could be bought by a white boy of means without any consideration of the short- or long-term consequences. It didn't occur to me either; I was actually thrilled when Nate bought me, handily, with the highest bid.

Nate was a junior pro skier and competed regularly on a regional team. On Slave Day, he made me wear his skin-tight, full-body, thick neoprene ski-racing suit, clunky ski boots, and ski goggles, while I carried his books from class to class. Other girls were instructed to wear Halloween costumes, or maybe a suit and tie that belonged to the father of their owner.

Clomping to class in our middle school model of a Southern plantation, I noticed a boy I'd never seen before.

"Who's that?" I asked my friend Jessie, who had been dressed in a nurse's uniform by her slave owner.

"Oh," she said, enraptured. "That's Hopper Tilson."

Tall, with a shock of white-blond hair and lucent blue eyes, Hopper sauntered through our middle school hallways like he could take or leave school, like it was ultimately useless but potentially amusing. Hopper had an older brother and an older sister, both as blond and arrestingly attractive as him. I almost choked on my own saliva when he said hello to me in the hallway a few days after I'd first noticed him.

Hopper's father, Henry, an established novelist and screenwriter, was born to a wealthy family in Birmingham, Alabama, where he was raised, and was the near spitting image of Warren Beatty. His wife, Rose, a multimedia artist, also from Birmingham, was a former Miss Alabama who had once dated Elvis Presley. They'd recently moved to a small town a few miles north of Warner to raise their three children, Silas, Tallulah, and Hopper, who each excelled at skiing and snowboarding and singing and acting and, above all else, being better than the rest of us, larger than their surroundings and effortlessly appealing. I was drawn to them in a narcotic way.

Their house, about twenty minutes away by car, was at the top of a back road off the highway and sat opposite a small pond surrounded by acres of grass. There was a garage turned personal gym where Henry worked out, and a tennis court behind the house. They had two golden retrievers, and the interior of their home was modern country glamorous, something you'd see in the pages of Town & Country magazine. Rose had a dressing room at the top of the stairs where all her clothes and shoes were housed, along with a vanity table with brooches and jewels in velvet boxes, ribbons and hats, feathers and her own shadow box art.

As with Ella, I asserted myself into the Tilson world because I wanted what they had. And, also like Ella, they were either charmed or impressed by my somewhat furtive moxie. With the Tilsons, though, my blackness seemed like an advantage, a way to be exceptional and interesting—nobody in their sphere was "common." Dinner guests included famous filmmakers, actors, and broadcast journalists. Tallulah had a picture in her room of herself at a party with Michael Jackson.

When we first became friends, Hopper would roller-skate the twelve miles or so to my house to hang out, and then later his father would pick him up in their Jeep Wagoneer with side paneling. Ours was a friendship that took place outside of school, where the popularity politics were rigid and irrelevant to Hopper's level of agency. Later, after I got my driver's license, I would drive myself to his house, and very often said little, immersing myself in their world and blending into the furniture as they played out this life that seemed fantastically unburdened, captivating, and casually luminous. Silas and Hopper were always making music out of weird things like window frames, kitchen utensils, or pot lids alongside a regular electric keyboard, while Tallulah, the lone girl child, tall and striking, exerted as much voice and vocals, either singing or just talking loudly, as she could.

One night on my way to the movies with Silas, Hopper, and Tallulah in the Jeep, windows open in the summertime at dusk, heading out on Route 103 just before the exit to Concord, I saw the outline of a tiny woman trailed by a medium-sized dog walking on the shoulder of the road. As we got closer, I could see the switch of her angry hips, a rabbit's-ear key chain dangling furiously from the belt loop of her stonewashed jeans. She flicked her cigarette out into the highway as we sailed by. It was Riana, with her dog Peaches, on the road to nowhere, while I was in a chariot with gods.

After that night she'd come home filled with rage, Riana started dating physically abusive boys, among them a boy named Scott, who once showed up at our house with a self-inflicted gunshot wound to his shoulder. She'd broken up with him, and he couldn't live without her, he said. Dad told me to go to bed while he dealt with Scott.

I pretended not to recognize my sister as we sailed past her on the highway. I was embarrassed by her. She looked like a redneck, or a prostitute trying to escape her john in some seedy R-rated movie. But seeing Riana walking along the highway alone at night, with cars flying by within feet of her small frame, which was not just stupid but dangerous, suddenly brought to bear the acute lack of guidance or structure we had in our family.

There was no grounding in culture or religion or aspiration. We were a family in cognitive disarray, empirical chaos—no one belonged to anyone. We lived in a castle with an absentee king. At the Tilson's house, Henry reveled in his Southern-style patriarchy, tapping both his daughter and his wife on the ass when they said something clever, and called smart, attractive women "good girls."

There was an ease, a merry nonchalance inside their home, an ongoing, rousing movement that felt like a movie set, with flaw- less performances, glamorous costumes, and the smartest, fun- niest dialogue. They had special pet names for one another, and laughed at one another's jokes. The children were the focus—how they grew and observed the world and succeeded; what they liked and loved—and I felt a sense of mourning for the loss of that same kind of focus from Mom and Dad when we were very small kids, up on Pumpkin Hill. A focus that had shifted abruptly after I'd met Tess, when it seemed they felt free to focus their attention elsewhere.

Hopper, like his brother and sister, went away to private school for high school, but whenever he was home for a holiday break, I'd invite myself over to visit with him and his family, suck in their rarified air, and fantasize that my blackness would always grant me such provisional gold-star approval.

✣ Sixteen ✣

I saw him only once. Usually when Tess went out with her "lover," a black man named Carl, she left to meet him somewhere in town, but tonight he'd come to pick her up. Since she'd split with Miguel three years before, Tess dated now and again, but her monthly night with Carl, she'd told me, was mostly just about sex.

"Well, hello," Carl said when I answered the door.

"Hi, I'm Rebecca," I said, welcoming him inside.

"Oh, I know who you are." He smiled. Carl's head nearly grazed the ceiling, and his voice was rich and slow, drawn out like a long summer day.

"You do?" I asked, surprised.

"Yes, of course," Carl lilted. "You're Tessie's daughter."

Tessie? Who the hell calls her Tessie? I thought. As if summoned, Tess suddenly appeared, flush from running down the stairs.

"OK, the boys are in bed, ready for you to read to them," she said, hurriedly. "Sebastian is not pleased that I'm going out, so you should head up now."

"OK," I said. "Have fun, nice meeting you, Carl."

"Nice meeting you, too, my dear," Carl said, putting his arm around Tess's shoulders to lead her out the door.

✣   ✣

Tess wore a sandalwood or similarly scented perfume. It wasn't overly strong, and I never actually saw her apply it, but I loved the smell, like bare skin, honey, and musk. With the boys asleep after I'd soothed Sebastian and read them both several bedtime stories, I went into Tess's room to find the small amber-colored vial on her dresser. I unscrewed the black cap, held the contents to my nose, and inhaled Tess's smell. The vial was tiny in between my fingers, and I was afraid I might drop it, but before I put the cap back on, I held my finger over the opening and gently flipped it so there was just a fingerprint of liquid that I drew across the inside of my wrist.

"Are you wearing my perfume?" Tess asked, moments after she arrived home that night. I'd only wanted it for me, so that I could keep her with me, inhale her smell when no one was looking.

"Yes, I just love the smell so much." I thought she might be flattered.

"Get your own essence," she scoffed. "And wash my perfume off. Everybody has their own essence, Rebecca. This one is mine, and you need to find your own." Her tone softened a bit, and I could tell she was trying to turn this into a teaching moment instead of yet another instance of what she saw as my shortcomings.

"Black men are the best lovers," Tess said the next day. "They have more rhythm, they just do. I highly recommend that your devirginizer be black."

I was fourteen years old and barely even thinking about sex but for the fact that Tess talked about sex *a lot* and had recently become obsessed with me losing my virginity.

"What about Troy?" she suggested. Troy was almost twenty years older than me, and the first black friend of Tess's that I'd met prior to Carl, who wasn't technically her friend but, rather, her "lover." Funny and kind, towering and geeky with thick, bottle-cap glasses, Troy adored Tess, and was gracious with me, although clearly uncomfortable when she made this suggestion to him in the living room a few days later.

"I don't think that's such a good idea," Troy said, laughing awkwardly. I sat on the floor nearby, against the wall facing the window, where the sun poured in on a bright afternoon in late spring, trying to look relaxed and maybe attractive? I wasn't sure what I was supposed to be doing in this dynamic, where Tess had invited Troy over to casually suggest he take my virginity. It was extremely weird and uncomfortable.

"I'm sure there's someone out there for you, Rebecca," Troy said, trying to keep things friendly, like this was all a silly joke. "Someone more age-appropriate maybe!"

Tess left the two of us sitting in an awkward silence while she went to make lunch.

"Come eat," she said after what seemed like an eternity. The subject of Troy as my "devirginizer" never came up again.

Back at Kearsarge, Ryan started dating his first serious girlfriend. Her name was Bliss, and she had brown doe-eyes and shoulder-length strawberry-blonde hair and bangs. She was a year behind us, and she was thin and perfect, and Ryan fell head over heels for her. He also immediately stopped talking to me. After pining over him for years now, I still thought somewhere in the back of my mind that he would come around to the idea of us being together, even though I also knew it was pretty unlikely.

It was crushing to watch the way he looked at Bliss, and I felt demoralized, stupid for thinking he would ever want me like that. Or that any of the white boys I went to school with would choose me over girls who reflected the images I saw every day in magazines, on TV, and in the movies, *everywhere*—Brooke Shields, Phoebe Cates, Cindy Crawford, Alyssa Milano, Molly Ringwald, Julia Roberts.

There were moments that evoked the same confusion I'd felt when Mrs. Gordon had told me I was pretty for a black girl, moments regarding my appearance and level of attraction that felt arbitrary, delusional, and always guided by an observation made by a white person. Like with Connor, who was a good friend, generous and thoughtful, an only child who wore the spoils of his privilege with a notable measure of resentment. He was tight with Nate and Ryan, and wore clean Stan Smith sneakers, white with Adidas's signature green heel tab, and straight cuffed chinos. He was the first white boy in high school to tell me outright that he thought I was pretty, but then he ignored me for the rest of the week.

Beyond that, attention from boys during high school came at a cost. Drunken white seniors made out with me just before passing out late at night at weekend kegger parties, or in a hot tub where everyone was getting high. One boy tried to rape me behind a closed door at a party once. He pushed a clothing bureau against the door once we were inside the room, turned out the light, and grabbed my arm, forcing me to sit down next to him on the single bed.

I heard him unzip his pants, and then let out a gasp when I felt his hand grab the back of my head and shove it down onto his erect penis. It was too awkward to stay seated next to him, so I had to kneel down in front of him with his hand still on my head. "Do it. I know you want it," he grunted, his fingers moving to clamp the base of my neck. "I saw you looking at me. I know you want this." His penis was rubbery in my mouth, warm and pulsing. I worried about my teeth. My chin skimmed the zipper of his pants, and I thought it might leave a scratch.

I *had* been looking at him. He was the star player on the opposing soccer team we'd defeated under the home field lights a few hours before. Blond and blue-eyed, athletic and cocksure, he was impossible to miss, and I wasn't the only girl watching him work the room. His arrogance in coming to a party with the team that had just defeated him was impressive, but he was also undeniably good-looking, and I could hardly believe it when he struck up a conversation with me out of all the other girls who were there.

"Let's explore this place, huh?" he'd said, his hand gently grazing my shoulder, the same hand that was now holding my head down. Tall, sweaty boys still in their soccer uniforms pumped the keg behind us, raucous and crowing from their win, as he led me into that tiny bedroom.

The bureau came crashing down just as I'd started to gag. "Oh my God, Becky!! Look at this mess! You need to clean all this up, right now! Oh my God!" Lisa had been one of the other girls looking at him. She barged into the room, mad that I was in there alone with him. She didn't see, or didn't want to see, that he was assaulting me.

A few weeks later, a very popular senior boy named Kurt who was captain of the soccer team and had either been at the party or heard about it, showed up at my house late at night. Built in the 1700s and barely altered since, our front door didn't have a proper lock. I don't even recall whether Mom and Dad were home, but if they were, they were asleep, and Kurt took the liberty of letting himself in.

We'd been friendly at school, but he was friendly with everyone. That was part of his persona—a beloved straight-A student who drove a red Jeep and went out with his female counterpart, an equally beloved, straight-A student, president of her class and of political programs and other extracurriculars and sports.

Kurt appeared in my bedroom, maybe tipsy, and got into my bed with me. I was startled, but also flattered, because Kurt, who might as well have been a local celebrity, was in my bed, with me. He rubbed up against me until his penis was hard under his pants, then moaned, stood up, and rearranged himself, smiling. "Look what you made me do," he said. And then left.

My body, I was learning, was a prop or a toy at the hands of my white male peers. A brown body to explore, pass around, and violate, but never to fall in love with or date.

Seventeen

"Nate, *come on, the prom is* so stupid anyway," I said, sipping from a can of Diet Pepsi at a table in the library. We were hanging out after school before his soccer practice started. "Dude, let's just go for the hell of it? Who cares?"

"Sure, why not?" Nate said, shrugging his shoulders. Nate and I had remained good friends since middle school, when I'd been his confidante and shoulder to cry on through numerous breakups with his then girlfriend Ella, who had left to spend a year abroad. Now Nate had just broken up with another girlfriend, Ginny, a few weeks before the sophomore prom, which, although it was widely considered pretty corny as a thing, a lot of popular couples still attended and used as an excuse to make out all night.

"We can dress up, it'll be fun," I said. "And we can leave early if we get bored."

After trying desperately to assimilate with the preppy crowd during middle school—saving babysitting money to buy pink and green Izod polo shirts, borrowing L.L. Bean sweaters from friends, and begging Catherine and Tess to buy me Nike sneakers—I'd gone in the complete opposite direction fashion-wise in high school, and now shopped almost exclusively at thrift shops. I modeled myself after Lisa Bonet's character Denise from *The Cosby Show*, wearing oversized men's blazers, harem pants, scarves and strips of lace tied around my head, button-up shirts, and large, beaded brooches pinned at the neck.

Recently I'd found a pair of men's black tuxedo tails and a short red strapless dress at a shop that had clearly just received a big drop from a cocktail-party-going crowd. *What better excuse to wear these two fancy pieces than the prom?* I thought.

"Sure," Nate said, if not enthusiastic then at least up for it. "I'll come pick you up, and you can dress me." Nate smiled, suddenly amused at the thought. "This will be fun. OK, gotta go to practice." He grabbed his stuff and got up to leave. "Later."

"Later," I said, feeling warmly toward Nate as I watched him walk down the hall toward the gym. Not in a romantic way, but I was overcome by an enormous sense of appreciation that he was my friend. There was nothing to read into; neither of us was harboring an unspoken crush or feeling an unrequited love toward the other. We weren't playing games. We were two sophomores in high school who had been friends since the sixth grade, and who thought it might be fun to dress up and go to the prom together. When he said he would come pick me up, there was no question in my mind that he would—I knew that he would show up for me, and that felt good.

Our inner circle of friends was small, so people found out pretty quickly that Nate and I had decided to go to the prom together. The next day when I walked into school, I was immediately besieged by concerned friends. Had I heard? they asked. Heard what?

"Nate's father forbid him to take you to the prom," my friend Mark said.

Forbid him? I thought. It's the prom. Whose parents *forbid* their child from going to the prom?

"What? Why?" That I didn't immediately connect the dots and

answer my own question is evidence that I was either delusional or hopeful regarding my viability and worth among my white peers. Especially since Nate's father, Mr. James, was my US history teacher, and had not so subtly indicated a few weeks prior that I was dumb because I'm black. It had been during a class when he was teaching us about the American economy, and Mr. James said something about how smart the early Southern settlers had been. I asked if he thought having slaves had made the settlers smart. "You don't even know what you're talking about," he snapped back at me. "You see, black people don't think right, and that's your problem."

"He said if Nate goes with you, he won't allow any pictures to be taken, because who wants to look back and see that you took a black girl to the prom?" Mark, tall and serious with an exceptionally defined jawline and near maniacally focused eyes, seemed both mortified and tantalized by this information. It was as though he felt honored to wield this very grown-up set of circumstances that we all knew was slightly horrifying, but had never heard of having happened before.

"Well, that sucks," I said, trying to shake it off, but it felt like my face was starting to dissolve, drips of brown flesh sliding down my cheekbones and landing onto my shoulders, pooling in messy dark blobs.

"Mr. James is an asshole," Mark said, in an effort to console me. As if Mr. James being an asshole made it easier for me to dismiss or unhear what I had just been told.

The words "who wants" and "a black girl" were attacking each other in my brain, gouging holes into the "girl," beating bruises onto the "black," wishing the "want" had a name before it, any name at all.

The school bell rang and it was time to go to class, the racism dissipating into the everyday ether for Mark and all of my white peers. Later, I asked Nate about it.

"Let's just go anyway," he said, standing in front of a wall of cubicles near the physics classroom. "Whatever. We don't have to take pictures." He thought he was being a good friend.

On the night of the prom, Nate stood admiring himself in front of the floor-length mirror in my bedroom. The vintage tuxedo tails fit him to a T. I joined him in the reflection, standing at his side, my bare brown collarbones and rounded shoulders rising up out from under the tight, bright red taffeta of my dress that fell just to the top of my knees. Nate grabbed his lapels, grinning like a showman, and I looped my arm inside the crux of his, smiling, too. Nate had beautiful, clear eyes and garnet-colored lips. He'd grown taller since middle school, and gone from boyish-looking to handsome. We looked amazing.

"OK, let's go!" Nate said, patting down his chest and the back pockets of his jeans for what I presumed to be his car keys.

"Didn't you just have them?" I said.

"I'm not looking for my keys, I'm looking for my wallet," he said, visibly annoyed. "Shit, I think I left it at home. Is it OK if we stop at my house real quick on the way?"

"I guess so," I said, deflated after such a sweet moment in front of the mirror, and irritated that we had to make a stop before getting to the school. The prom started at seven, and it was already close to eight.

"It'll be really quick, I promise. Unless you want to pay for PC's," Nate said, playfully. "PC's" was short for Peter Christian's, a rustic, pub-like restaurant close to school where a bunch of us often gathered for chips and dip or grasshopper brownie chip pie after parties or soccer games. Nate and I thought we'd probably bail the prom early and meet up with friends there.

"OK, fine," I said, knowing that I couldn't afford to pay for PC's even if I'd wanted to.

I don't think Nate realized it until we pulled into his driveway, when he turned off the engine, looked over at me in the passenger seat, and then turned the engine back on.

"Um, I'll just leave the car running so you can stay warm," he said awkwardly, as if he weren't hiding me from his father. "I'll just be a minute, I promise."

I watched him walk up the driveway to his house, the head-lights exposing him as fully as I was hidden inside the dark car, set against the pitch-black night, with the heat on. Part of me wanted to jump out of the car and march up behind Nate, blast through the door, and just stand in front of Mr. James. But the other, more familiar part of me sat isolated and stuck inside my own chaotic unease about my identity. Because even though Nate had defied his father's racist warning, I was still unworthy of being seen, of being remembered as part of a major moment in Nate's young life, in *our* young lives.

A few minutes later, Nate bounded out of the house, back down to the car. He got in, looked over at me, pretending that he hadn't just hidden me from his father, and said, "Ready?"

"Yeah," I said. "OK." But I couldn't get back that feeling I'd felt when I'd watched him walk down the hallway toward practice that day after school, when we'd first decided to go to the prom together, or that moment in the mirror less than an hour before, when he grinned and I smiled, and we were two friends who had dressed up together for a special night of silly fun.

Nate backed out of the driveway, and we drove to the school in silence. Inside the gym was dark, the vibe was lackluster and lazy, punch bowls half full and popcorn spilled all over tables and the floor underneath. Students were coupled off in dark corners, or swaying arm in arm as the longest slow-dance song in the history of slow-dance songs, "Stairway to Heaven," crawled out of the speakers. We were later than we'd mentioned we might be to friends, and now couldn't see anyone we'd planned to meet up with.

"You OK?" Nate asked. I was standing against the wall with my arms crossed.

"Yeah, I'm fine. I don't really feel like staying here, though. You?"

"Want to go back to your house?" Nate said, suddenly shifting from my good friend to a random, horny teenager.

We were definitely just friends, but once in the seventh grade when we'd snuck out of a school play to talk about his most recent breakup with Ella, Nate kissed me abruptly and then asked if he could touch my breasts. He hadn't pushed himself on me in a forceful way, more in an entitled way that made me feel like a blow-up doll he could fool around with when no one else was watching. When I said no about touching my boobs, the face he made then was the same face he was making now—as if it were my loss.

And I did feel a loss, but it wasn't the opportunity to fool around with my friend; it was the loss of innocence about how my white friends saw me, or didn't see me.

"Why is everything suddenly all about race for you?" Nate said a couple of weeks after the prom. He was annoyed that I kept bringing it up, along with how insane it was to me that his father, our US history teacher, had reacted the way he had to us going together.

"How can it not be about race when there's no other reason for something?" I said.

"Something like what?" Nate said, leaning against the wall near the gym after school.

"Like your father *telling* you that you won't want to look back in pictures and see that you took a black girl to the prom. That black girl is me, Nate!"

"I mean, I guess. But he's from another time, you know?"

"Nate, you should have heard what he said to me in class a few weeks ago."

"I don't really want to know, OK? Look, you're my friend. Why can't we just leave it at that?"

"Maybe you can, but I can't," I said, frustrated.

"I gotta go to practice. Later," Nate said, and left.

✢ Eighteen ✢

I watched in the mirror as giant clumps of hair fell to the floor around me.

I hadn't kept up with Ida's hair-care instructions to keep my scalp greased, or to wrap it at night, or to wear a bonnet to bed, the last of which didn't even make sense to me. But even if I'd understood her instructions properly, I lacked the discipline to apply them. Tess reasoned that if I didn't know or want to learn how to take care of my hair, and since no one else within a forty-mile radius of Warner knew how either, I should just get it all chopped off. "It'll be low-maintenance, and super chic," she said, and for my fifteenth birthday, she took me to a glitzy, high-profile salon in downtown Portsmouth called 210, where you had to make appointments weeks in advance.

I didn't just not know how to take care of my hair; I had grown to hate it. I felt antagonized by its texture and unavoidable otherness. It wouldn't stay or hold or shine or fall. I couldn't tuck it behind my ears like all the white girls in school did with their straight, shiny hair, or casually flip it over my shoulder, run my fingers through it, or brush it out of my eyes.

Tess and I brought a picture of the black actress Shari Belafonte we'd torn out of a magazine to use as an example of the look we were going for. Belafonte, the daughter of iconic actor Harry

Belafonte, had successfully transitioned from modeling to acting in the '80s and was known for her short, crop-cut afro.

In the sleek styling chair across from a mirror that ran the length of the wall, surrounded by track lights and pop music, I watched the stylist as she wielded a pair of cutting shears to lop off my hair, leaving clumps of frizz on the floor. I felt a minute of regret, and also of guilt, as if I was disrespecting all the work that Ida had done, the distinct and particular care she had taken years before, when no one else in my life did or could. Mom had met us there, because it was a very big deal, and also, she had been visiting with her parents, my grandparents, and would drive us home after my haircut.

I watched Mom in the mirror as she stood next to me sitting in the stylist's chair. "It's so beautiful, Beck," she said, almost mournfully. "So soft-looking. Maybe you should leave it at that length."

We were about midway through the cut, my hair about the length it was when I still wore it as a big, free afro when I was little. Mom turned to Tess, who was seated in the waiting area with a mirage of distance. "Don't you think it's just gorgeous at this length, Tess?"

Tess shrugged her shoulders. "I think it will look more chic when it's real short," she said, looking at me instead of Mom. "Don't you think, Rebecca?"

I nodded.

"Hold still," the perky stylist said.

Over the phone when I'd gotten back to Warner after my hair cut, Tess expressed her concern over the way she thought Mom had romanticized my hair.

"It's just hair, Rebecca. Your mother, and your father, too, see you as this exotic being," Tess said, again, in part of a mini-lecture that had become routine. "You're not any more special than any other kid," she said. "You've said that they remind you, far too often in my opinion, of how beautiful you are, but do they care about your education? Have they put any money aside for you to attend college?"

I tried to explain to Tess that they were artists, and we very rarely, if ever, talked about things like education or college savings. We didn't even have health insurance.

"But you do talk to them about their love affairs, right?"

Yes, I told her, especially with Dad, because we were close; he confided in me.

"Frankly, I think you're *too* close with your father," she said. "And your mother is hobbled by her husband."

If Tess thought Mom was hobbled by Dad, Mom thought Tess hated men. Tess was independent and opinionated, strident even; she had a job that she went to every day; she could take or leave a partner, while Mom couldn't imagine her life without Dad and deferred to him on almost everything. She rarely espoused serious, forthright opinions on anything outside of the house, and she'd never held a regular job, which Tess often brought up.

"Your mother has never had to work for a living, and that's why she follows the lead of your father. She has no character of her own. Working builds character," Tess said, during another phone conversation.

"All Dad cares about is Catherine anyway," I said, glumly.

Dad and Catherine had started to collaborate as creative partners by illustrating the pottery Catherine's husband threw, and were regularly touring the New England craft show circuit together.

"I wish I was with you, I hate it here," I said. When I wasn't at school, I was often home alone, and I'd started to feel extremely lonely and stuck, parented mostly by the TV and occasional, distant, and not-quite-maternal missives from Tess over the phone. Warner had begun to seem limited in the extreme, and I longed more and more to be near Tess, and the livelier small-city setting of Portsmouth.

"Well, try not to *hate* it, Rebecca. But I wish you were here, too," Tess said.

I'd never heard her say this before, and it marked an enormous shift in our relationship. I felt like a different person when I was with Tess, when we spoke on the phone, and it finally felt like being the daughter of her making was within reach. I could mimic the sound of her voice, echo her opinions, side with her against my parents, laugh like her, dress like her, smoke cigarettes in the attic—Merit Ultra Lights, the same brand that Tess smoked.

I folded into the mere sound of Tess's voice, dizzying, liquid, and lethal like freebase cocaine shimmering in its heated spoon. It was an electric sensation, not like the safe, smooth feeling of Mom's love, and I chose it outright.

Telling Tess that I hated being in Warner was the crack that she needed in what she perceived as the veneer of the happy, special adopted child, and her tenor changed almost overnight. We became inseparable, finishing each other's sentences, creating an invisible and impenetrable protectiveness around us at all times when we were together. Our relationship took up acres of space, giant swaths of air that moved at the pace of a tornado, in the eye of which we twirled around together like tireless, unbowed dance partners.

I surrendered to Tess as if doing so would somehow lift or reverse her surrender *of* me when I was a baby. She was hard on me, but she was also funny and charismatic and brilliant. From her I learned concepts and phrases like "power differential" and "situational ethics" and "full dance card" and "self-awareness" and "chances are slim and none, and Slim just took off." Erudite expressions like "glib repartee" and "modus operandi" and "fait accompli" and "bon mot."

"Have you thought about what you might like to do with your life?" Tess asked, one morning, while we sat on the couch in her living room, with bottles of Poland Spring water.

"I feel like, maybe an actress?" I said, smiling, because I felt both serious and not serious about it, and also because I knew Tess would have a strong opinion about it either way.

"Do you want to be an actress, Rebecca, or do you want to be famous?" Tess said, raising her eyebrows like she did when she wanted me to know I'd slipped.

I sat with that for a minute.

"I mean, they're kind of the same thing, right?"

"No, Rebecca," she said, and I could hear the exasperation that used to regularly show up in her voice, that I hadn't heard in months, maybe even a year.

"Listen, Miss Rebecca." Tess's "black" affect meant I wasn't going to hear this from anyone else, so I'd better stay focused. "Aspiring for that kind of attention is fucked up. Something is real wrong with you if that's what you want or feel like you need."

"You're right," I said. "That was dumb. Just kidding!"

And then we laughed about the idea, but it felt like we were laughing at me.

We had both adored and devoured popular culture long before we met, and watching the Oscars together either over the phone or in person became a celebrated annual tradition. We loved all awards shows, including the Emmys and the Grammys, during which Tess never missed an opportunity to comment on the acceptance speeches of winning black artists: "They loooooove to thank *Jesus!*" But the Oscars were special.

We indulged in all manner of chocolate, and talked nonstop about the hairstyles and gowns, who looked like what and was clearly dating whom, who gave the best performances, because we'd always seen all the movies nominated, who should win what and the spectacle of it all, event television at its finest. We were petty and catty and judgy in the pre–*Gawker*, Borowitz Report '80s, before the popularization of highbrow critical snark. Sometimes we'd perform our commentary throughout the whole broadcast in our Valley girl accents, which we started to affect after seeing the movie starring Nicolas Cage.

Tess read *People* magazine religiously, and I followed suit. We interpreted the meaning of songs as inside jokes, honing our sarcasm in lockstep. "What do you think they mean when they say 'push it'?" Tess said, of Salt-N-Pepa's hit 1986 anthem. "Maybe, like, a grocery cart?" I'd respond, feigning obliviousness, as if we were doing a stand-up comedy bit.

We watched Richard Gere movies until our eyes went cross, and obsessed over the sex scene between Jeff Bridges and Rachel Ward in *Against All Odds*, hot and dark and breathless in the ruins of Cozumel, Mexico. We packed up trashy magazines, quart-sized Poland Spring seltzers, low-SPF bottles of sunscreen or none at all, and two beach chairs to settle in for full days at the beach to keep up "tan maintenance," as Tess called it. I felt closer to her when I bronzed up into a nice nut brown instead of wintertime's sallow light-skinned black.

Tess's favorite Stevie Wonder song was "Golden Lady," with "Knocks Me Off My Feet" a close second, and maybe tied with second "Ribbon in the Sky." That was our song. She knew exactly what she would and wouldn't do, and had the most resonant laugh I'd ever heard, a trill of radical self-possession, clipped girlhood, and feral, territorial bliss. She was a self-declared feminist, a term or thing I didn't even know existed before we met, and the only adult in my life who pointed out that what was happening in the 1984 cult classic *Purple Rain* was domestic violence, between the parents of Prince's character, the Kid, and between the Kid and Apollonia. Leah and I had only been obsessing previously, like everyone else, over how thrillingly sexy and dangerous Prince's performance was in the film, which we watched on VCR when it came to video.

When Tess's light shone on me, it was hypnotizing. *You look young, bright, strong . . . as if you are awakening to something of which you are (will be) in total possession. Could this be your SELF? I don't know. But you hum with hope,* she wrote in a letter to me. I *felt* like I was humming with hope—her hope in me.

It was a love affair of the highest order, an unsupervised joyride into the depths of what could have been, me back into the womb, bathed in her mercurial amniotic fluid, imagining that she might rub her belly with pride, no longer pretending I wasn't there as she had the first time. She would push and strain in labor and keep me this time, forever.

Nineteen

As I watched the boys pop and lock, it reminded me of that sixth grade assembly years before, when the black break-dancer had looked at me longingly before I turned away from him. This group of dancers—the Apple Jam Crew—was performing at Prescott Park in Portsmouth on a summer day when I was fifteen years old. This time, I knew I would not turn away. They spun and dipped their bodies with such mesmerizing joy, it felt like I was experiencing the feeling of desire for the first time. My long, unrequited crush on Ryan was certainly about a physical attraction—I definitely wanted to kiss him, a lot—but I had never felt this kind of visceral longing before.

Tess and my brothers sat on the grass nearby, allowing me this moment alone, as I stood out front among the rest of the audience. One boy with a baby face and oval brown eyes smiled at me, and I smiled back. We locked eyes, and after the performance I stayed behind as others wandered off with their small children—some you could tell were tourists, others just locals spending some time at the park, taking in the glorious public gardens with its red and gold and purple flowers in seasonal glow.

He walked toward me, sly and cocksure, while the other boys folded up their cardboard and packed up their gear. The boom box was still playing, and kids of various ages who had gathered to watch kept moving to the beat, twirling and shaking their little hips, trying to spin on their backs, impeded by the grass.

"You go to the Speakeasy?" he asked, before even saying hello.

"What?" I said.

"My name's Doug, but my crew name's Ice Cube—my boys call me Cube." This was pre–N.W.A, pre–famous rapper Ice Cube.

"Oh, hey. I'm Rebecca," I said, eager to hear him say something else.

"Cool, cool. Rebecca. OK."

As soon as I heard Cube speak, I wondered for the first time what my birth father's voice might sound like. How would it sound to hear him say my name? Would he have the same cadence as Cube? Was my birth father's manner of speaking fluid or halting? Was his meter casual or pointed, separated by quiet pauses or sprinkled throughout with "ums" or "you knows"? Would it sound black like Cube's or black like mine? Was my voice even black? There was no one who modeled a black male voice in my immediate life, no black male sound that spoke to me with warm affection, a familial melody. Until now.

"What's the Speakeasy?"

Cube explained it was a nearby dance club that held an under-twenties night every Wednesday and Sunday. I felt a thrilling wave of relief. Dance was a language I felt fluent in, a vernacular I could rely on. *I got this*, I thought. Cube and I said goodbye, and I found Tess, brimming with excitement. I told her about this place called Speakeasy and asked her if she would take me the next Sunday.

"We'll have to find a sitter for the boys, but I think we can figure something out." Tess gave me a look of encouragement and shared excitement.

✢ ✤

When Sunday arrived, Tess helped me pick out what to wear, something white and billowy made out of nylon parachute material. She let me use her powder blush that came in a small brick red earthen pot, and was applied with a squat brush with a round wooden handle. Just a touch on the cheekbones, a bit of mascara and gloss.

In the kitchen of her apartment I leaned against the sink, visibly nervous. The boys had gone to bed, and a friend would come over to stay with them as they slept so that Tess could drive us to the Speakeasy. I didn't have a driver's license yet, and there were no cell phones, no internet, no Ubers or Lyfts back then. The thought of my taking a cab by myself would have been ridiculous, in terms of both cost and safety.

"Here," Tess said, reaching up above the sink behind me to pull a bottle of Grand Marnier out of the cupboard. "Have a shot of this, it will calm your nerves." The only other time I'd tasted hard liquor was when Dad gave me a tiny sip of his special Italian liqueur, Galliano, which was a syrupy bright yellow and tasted of licorice.

The Grand Marnier felt hot and sharp going down my throat, but then smoothed out, and my arms loosened their grip across my chest. I felt relaxed on the car ride over, the tight curls of my newly shorn crop cut slick, doused with some hair product that the white women at 210 had given me—packaged differently and far more expensive than the slim brown pump bottle of Sta-Sof-Fro Ida had given me years before.

The Speakeasy was a former roller-skating rink in Portsmouth, about a twenty-minute drive from Tess's apartment, and the under-twenties night started at eight o'clock, just as it began to get dark in the summertime. A line of young people, almost entirely black, spilled from the entrance into the mostly vacant parking lot. I felt both unnerved and beckoned by it. A few white girls with long nails and bright blue eye shadow stood out, hands on their hips, pushing out their bottoms to add curves where there were none.

Tess and I joined the line, the two of us an odd pairing, though at thirty-two, Tess still could have easily passed for early twenties. There were no other such pairings; the few white girls stood together, and the rest, a swath of blackness, vibrated with the natural energy of freedom.

Inside, Tess fell back and sat at one of the small tables at the front, where she watched from afar, smoking and nursing a seltzer. She'd offered to stay, and I'd said OK, because I wanted her to see that I could handle myself with a boy who had shown an interest in me. I wasn't the passive eleven-year-old at the bar who didn't know how to fend off the advances of a sleazy older man anymore.

The dance floor was dark and pulsating with colorful strobes, while bass-heavy music rippled across the floor and ricocheted off the ceiling. It felt like heaven, and I was so immediately caught up in the ease and pleasure of it that it took half the night before I realized how out of my league I was when it came to dancing. Everyone else was flexing moves like the Running Man and the Cabbage Patch, and I was just moving to the music like I always had, while also looking around to see if I could spot Cube.

I danced alone, wondering if Cube was going to show up, before I realized that everyone else was dancing together, in small groups or in twos, syncing their moves and bumping their hips, arms raised, hands in the air, a kind of community and kinship I'd never seen or felt among my white peers back at high school. I went from surfing this wave of bliss to drowning in discontent, and started to think that maybe we should leave when Cube and his boys from the Apple Jam Crew took to the floor. It was exciting to see them arrive as a group, serious and intent, like an all-star team showing up to the court for a big game.

Soon they were joined by another break-dancing group, who wore their name, the Poppin' Express, on black T-shirts with bright red letters. I felt euphoric, as a spotlight splashed on from above and the boys started their dance-off, a battle of locks and freezes and backspins.

The leader of the Poppin' Express was about my age and dangerously beautiful. Tall and muscular, with dark skin and kingly eyes, he had a cool, seamless, measured style of dancing. He exuded confidence, and I actually ached watching him move. I watched him all night, standing as close as I could get in the circle surrounding their dance-off, wondering who he was.

"I saw you looking at that young Negro boy with that perfect heinie of his," Tess said on the drive home.

I giggled in the passenger seat next to her.

"Oh my God, Tess. He's so—"

"*Sexy!* Right? More sexy than he's got any damn business being."

"I loved watching him dance," I said, swooning.

"That's Kevin Davis," Tess said, passing along her in-the-know gossip gleefully.

"How do you even know his name?" I asked.

"It's a small town, Rebecca."

The next time at the Speakeasy, I spotted Kevin immediately standing in line with a white girl, posing arm in arm like the pictures you see of celebrity couples in *People* or *Us Weekly*. She casually tilted her head back and surveyed the rest of us, as if we were all waiting to see her. She looked like Ella and all the popular girls from Kearsarge, preppy and rich and pretty.

"That's that bitch Susie, from Oyster River," I heard a black girl say to another black girl, both standing in front of me on line. "She thinks she's better than everyone else, but she a hoe like the rest of them white hoes on Kevin's jock."

"*Girl*," the friend said. "You know he is *fine*, though."

"Of course her name is Susie," Tess said, at the kitchen table when we got home that night. We'd left early after seeing Kevin with Susie, who was clearly his girlfriend. They hadn't left each other's side for the three songs we'd stayed for.

"And you know damn well he's dating her *because* she's white."

"It just sucks," I said, feeling melodramatic.

"And you know he just *loves* how it looks to be on her arm," Tess said authoritatively. "Your birth father was the same way— *loved* to be paraded around by white women, like some handsome black buck."

I had no idea how to respond to this.

"So Kevin can prove to the other young Negro boys that he can get a white girl, and Susie can use him to make it seem like she's not a prude, which she almost definitely is. She looks so uptight, doesn't she? Repressed. Like, Susie has most definitely never been laid," Tess continued.

"I guess. But *girl*," I said, "he is fine, though."

Tess suddenly looked at me quizzically.

"What?" I said.

"Since when did you start saying 'girl' and 'fine'?"

"I've heard you say both of those words!" I said, defensively.

"It sounds disingenuous when you say it," Tess said, getting up from the table. "I'm going to bed. See you in the morning. Remember I have to leave early for work tomorrow, so you'll have the boys until Miguel can come to get them."

I started to pick up on a bizarre pattern, where not only did

Tess give herself permission to imitate her idea of blackness, but she also undermined my expressions of *being* black.

Despite my initial disappointment over the revelation of Susie, I went back to the Speakeasy again the next week. It was the last under-twenties night before school started back up, and that night, Kevin showed up alone, without Susie. I'd come alone, too. Tess had agreed to drop me off and meet up with a friend at a bar nearby until it was time to pick me up. I'd learned a few of the mainstream moves to faster music, to funky songs like Midnight Star's "Freak-A-Zoid" and "No Parking on the Dance Floor," but still mostly waited it out for the slower songs, when I was often asked to dance by a different black boy, whose weight and smell and skin I could sink myself into.

"All This Love" by DeBarge came on, and I saw Kevin, shoulders balanced, with a restrained swagger, walking directly toward me where I was standing off to the side of the dance floor. I thought I might die. He held his hand out to me and led me onto the floor, where spinning spots of light set a romantic stage. I was basking in his amazing scent, melon and soap and butter. I rested my cheek against his chest and wrapped my arms around his firm, narrow waist.

He pulled me in and whispered, "I been seeing you here." As if he hadn't shown up with his girlfriend the week before. As if he didn't have a girlfriend at all. Maybe they broke up, I hoped.

We danced together for the rest of the night, with him holding me, his hands spread across my lower back like a net I could fall into. Time disappeared until a tall, stunning black girl interrupted us and told him it was time to go.

"Ma is here, come on," she said, and then turned to me. "Hey, sis, I'm Jazmine."

"Hey," I said. "I'm Rebecca."

"Come on, Kevin, we gotta go."

Kevin nodded at his sister and then looked down at me, deep into my eyes. He was a boy of few words, which made him even more mysterious, appealing, and dreamy.

"See you around," he said, softly, and walked off in the direction his sister had gone.

How would I see him around? School was starting back up soon, and I'd get to Portsmouth less than I did in the summertime. We hadn't exchanged numbers—he didn't ask for mine, and I was too nervous to ask for his. But he'd said "See you around" like he meant it, before disappearing into the crowd. And I believed him.

Twenty

I'd never flown in an airplane before, and Connor, in the seat next to me, laughed as I flipped out over the smooth clip of the metal safety buckles, the efficiency of tray tables, and the thick in-flight magazine in the seat pocket in front of me. I turned the knobs over my head and pushed the window shade up and down like a four-year-old. I squealed during takeoff, and asked if the complimentary peanuts were free.

We were on our way to a weeklong politics program called Close Up, which offered high school students from all over the country the opportunity to use Washington, DC, as a classroom as a way to learn about how the government works. It cost a lot of money to go, but I qualified and was selected for a scholarship. Connor and I were among the small group attending from Kearsarge, but we didn't know the names of the other high schools that students were coming from until we arrived at the check-in center, which was packed with students standing abuzz in groups and different lines, carrying backpacks and holding folders of information, wearing lanyard ID badges around their necks.

My stomach dropped when I saw Kevin and Jazmine across the room, standing under a sign that read *Portsmouth High School.* I remembered Kevin's words—"See you around"—from a few weeks before at the Speakeasy, and immediately thought it was fate, that it was meant to be. How could he have known? I knew that he went to Portsmouth High School, because another girl I was sort of friendly with at the Speakeasy told me, but he almost certainly didn't know where I went to high school, not least of all because I generally lied about my background to the black boys I met at the Speakeasy. It had just been easier to say I lived in Portsmouth with my single white mother, and went away to private school in another part of New Hampshire for the rest of the year. That accounted both for my light skin and the funny way I talked.

I didn't say anything to Kevin at check-in, but I managed to make eye contact with him, and we smiled; he gave me a suave nod. Jazmine saw me, too, and smiled knowingly. Connor saw the silent exchange between me and Kevin, but wasn't feeling quite as charitable about it as Jazmine.

"Who's that?" he asked.

"Just this guy from Portsmouth," I said.

"Oh. Portsmouth," Connor replied. "Where you live your double life."

I thought I'd done a pretty good job at keeping the two worlds separate, out of necessity and for the sake of my sanity, but it was true that I would come back from visits in Portsmouth with a different sensibility, a sureness that rejected the social landscape at Kearsarge. It lasted only a few days before I was then wrested back into the provincial etiquette of daily popularity contests, dismissed and quietly denigrated at the whim of my white peers. On the one hand, Portsmouth and Tess bolstered my confidence, despite Tess's uneven attention and often bruising comments. But when I was at the pace that she set for us, it felt like being high.

✢ ✢

In the hallway at the hotel in DC, I ran into Jazmine and her girls outside their room, the ajar door allowing a glimpse of their open suitcases with hot-pink tops and strappy sandals, hair products and bunched-up satin bonnets spread out on their beds.

"Hey, girl," said Jazmine, statuesque and slender, curvy in all the right places. "Rebecca, right?"

I nodded. "Yeah," I said, trying to stay cool, hyperconscious of how my voice would probably come out sounding white to her.

"Where's your room at?"

"End of, ah, the hallway," I said. "With the rest of, y'know, the white people in my school." I hadn't planned to say that, but I *had* started to think about being surrounded by so many white people on the day-to-day.

Jazmine laughed. "Nah," she said. "We can't let you go out like that, sis. You should stay with us in our room. Go get your stuff and come through."

I tried to pretend that this open embrace by black girls didn't feel like the best thing that had ever happened to me.

"Yo," she said before I turned to go get my stuff. "You know there's a talent show the last night? You should perform with us."

"I'd love that," I said, before changing up my tone. "I mean, that'd be real cool, yeah. I'll go get my stuff."

Moving into Jazmine's room with her girls felt like moving out of my brain and into my body. The first full day of the program, we all sat together for lunch in a huge dining hall, where Jazmine and I compared schedules to see which classes and tours and events we would be at together, deciding to blow off the ones that didn't coincide. Once or twice I caught Connor looking at me from the table where he was sitting with other Kearsarge students before quickly turning away.

The second day, Jazmine and I were in a group with other black students in front of the Jefferson Memorial while a tour guide told us when it was built, and how Thomas Jefferson was a founding figure of the Democratic Party, and why he was so important, most of which we only pretended to listen to. Kevin was there, too, but had so far kept his distance, and I didn't press it, choosing to focus more on my budding friendship with Jazmine.

"Yo," said Desmond, another student from Portsmouth High. "Didn't Thomas Jefferson have slaves, though?"

"Everyone had slaves, you knucklehead," Jazmine said.

"Ain't that some shit." Desmond shook his head. "And who you callin' a knucklehead, Jazmine?"

"*You*, knucklehead!" Jazmine said, and they both fell out laughing.

"That ain't right," Desmond said, shaking his head, still laughing. "Yo, Kev, come get your little sis! She playing too much!" Desmond spoke loudly enough for Kevin to hear from where he was standing a few feet away. Kevin shook his head, and made an expression like Desmond was really just full-on wasting his time. I looked back and forth between them, laughing along with everyone else now, before pausing on Kevin, who gestured for me to come over. I tried not to run.

As the group moved toward the next monument, Kevin grabbed for my hand and didn't let go for the rest of the day. I was in heaven.

"Girl, she don't even like black people," Jazmine said when I asked her about Susie that night in our hotel room.

"Why is she dating Kevin then? But also, why is he dating *her*?"

"'Cause he thinks she's smart, and he likes smart girls. That's probably why he likes you."

"You think he likes me?"

"The hell you think he was holding your hand all day, fool!"

The other girls, their straightened hair tucked under bonnets for the night, were brushing their teeth, applying face cream, and riffling through their suitcases in the background, a swirling hive of black-girl movement, humming and sacred, while Jazmine and I sat on her bed and talked.

"She looks like a total snob," I said.

"Oh, girl, she's a bitch. I hate her," Jazmine said. "I wish Kevin would just break up with her already, because she plays with his emotions, you know? Like one day she calls and is pushing all up on him, then she don't answer *his* calls the next day."

"That sounds really—" I started.

"White?" one of the other girls chimed in from the bathroom. "Girl, you know her parents ain't trying to let her date no black boy."

"But she stay sweatin' him, because the Poppin' Express be hot right now," another girl said.

"I'd rather he was with you," Jazmine said. "And I'm gonna tell him tomorrow."

"I *really* like him," I said, hoping my admission might further encourage her to tell Kevin he should break up with Susie and be with me.

For the rest of the week, Kevin and I acted like a couple. We held hands most of the time, and he kept his arm around me while we sat together for the final dinner at a tavern in Colonial Williamsburg. But the next day, the last day of the program, he seemed to avoid me.

"He's just buggin' out," Jazmine assured me. "Wait till he sees you tonight."

We'd rehearsed all week for the talent show performance—a dance and lip-sync routine to "In My House" by the Mary Jane Girls. Jazmine had picked the song and done most of the choreography, based largely on the *Soul Train* video for the song, but allowed for me to chime in, given my six years of experience with the Rowland School of Dance, which I'd shared with my new girlfriends who thought it was "dope."

Jazmine, as the lead, wore a white blazer and pants, just like Mary Jane Girls' lead singer Joanne "JoJo" McDuffie did in the video that I'd seen on BET at Tess's. We didn't get BET in Warner. The rest of us, the backup girls, wore different brightly colored tops and tight skirts (I borrowed both from Jazmine), sparkly pink lip gloss, fierce black eyeliner and long-lash mascara, and big gold earrings, which again I had to borrow from Jazmine, having only brought along my thin silver hoops, the same style and make that Tess wore and which she allowed me to wear in tribute.

I was nervous, not because I didn't know the routine or the words, but because I knew that Kevin would be watching.

"Sing right to him, girl," Jazmine said before we went out on stage to perform.

The music came on through the speakers at the far side of the stage just behind the curtain, and we did our thing under a giant fake disco ball suspended from the ceiling. Jazmine was out in front with her long arms waving, enticing the audience as she did the snake, her body an *S* in white, while the girls and I stayed in rhythm, stepping to the left, to the right, leaning back and bending forward. It was more fun than I'd maybe had in my entire life, and the audience went wild as we took our bow together.

At the dance after the show, Kevin held me close and said, in his seductively subdued way, "You were real cute up there."

"Thanks," I said, snuggling into his chest and his smell.

"When you coming back to Portsmouth?" he asked.

"I'm not sure, but soon I hope."

"Yeah, me, too," Kevin said, taking my chin in his hand before bending down to kiss me.

Connor sat in the seat in front of me on the plane back home. I kicked the seat a few times to try to get his attention, but he ignored me, and didn't say goodbye at the airport when we arrived back in Boston, or offer me a ride back home. He'd driven his own car and given me a ride to the airport at the start of the trip, but now he wouldn't even look at me.

In between classes at school our first day back, I stopped him. "Hey, what's up?"

"Nothing," Connor said curtly. "I have to get to class."

"Wait, seriously, what's going on?" I pressed.

"I didn't realize you liked that guy so much. Do you even know him?"

I responded, channeling Jazmine, "Man, you buggin'."

Connor looked at me incredulously. "Oh, what? You're black now? Just because you dance with some black dude? Whatever."

That was the thing. I *was* black now. But I'd always been black; it's just that no one around me ever really saw me.

Twenty-One

Tess had just two pictures of my birth father, whose name I learned was Joe Banks. She gave them to me when I finally worked up the nerve to ask her, not long after I started going to the Speakeasy, spending time with black boys who had black fathers.

The week I'd spent in DC had emboldened me to lay claim to a biological parent, a lineage, and a history that would allow me to keep the joy I felt with Jazmine and Kevin and the other black kids as my own. But I needed to see it in my birth father's face and skin and posture, to take his image and existence out from the filter of Tess's subterfuge. The photos would allow me to piece together my own distillation of who my father was, and who he might be now.

Tess laid them out on the kitchen table, and I touched the worn edges as if they were velvet and not the creased, yellowing paper of pictures taken from another time. They appeared both vintage and modern, simultaneously relics and urgent pieces of evidence.

"They're yours to keep," Tess said.

I couldn't take my eyes off them.

One photo, in black and white, featured Tess and Joe in a wooded area, at a bit of a distance. Joe is in profile, leaning up against a tree, tall and narrow-looking with chiseled cheekbones, extending a thin branch of some sort to Tess, whose hand is reaching out to receive it. He's wearing a light-colored safari-style jacket and fitted pants hemmed at the ankle, wearing loafers, dark sunglasses and a short, tight afro. Tess, in jeans and white sneakers, has on a hooded windbreaker, her shoulder-length hair is pulled back in a low ponytail, and her mouth is ajar, as if she's saying something to Joe.

"I think I may have been pregnant with you in this one," she said.

"Really?"

"That looks like the fall, and I got pregnant with you in August. I mean, I wouldn't have known I was pregnant because I was in total denial," Tess said. It was something she'd said before, but I'd already gone back into the pictures, immersed in the images of my black father, suddenly feeling deeply attached to him.

The second photo, this one in color but also of the two of them, is more close-up, with Tess and Joe sitting on the grass among friends, at a political rally of some sort, Tess told me. Joe, again in profile, is wearing the same cargo jacket from the other picture, the same dark sunglasses, leaning back on his arms, looking forward, nose sloping down toward his lips. Tess is looking straight at the camera, her hair down and tucked behind her ears, wearing regular glasses and a denim jacket.

"Joe loved to be seen," Tess said. "And he was cool as a cuke."

"He looks it," I said. "I wish you had a picture of him without the sunglasses."

"Oh, he wore those sunglasses all the time. It was part of his appeal. He was very stylish, and veeeeery into his looks."

I had never heard Tess say more than four words about my birth father—"Basically, he was a dog"—and so this felt exciting, if also slightly unsettling. Why now? I didn't dare ask. I just wanted to sit with the photos and write a story in my head about me and my black father.

I wondered what he would say to me about these black boys I found so appealing all of a sudden. Would he call them jive, young Negro boys, as Tess had called more than one of them? Would he caution me to stay away from them, or tell me exactly how to handle them, and myself as his daughter?

"Do you know if I was his only daughter?" I asked.

"I don't, but you know black men are often out here having kids with a lot of different women. So who knows?" As soon as she said that, I lost the thread, and the story I was writing shifted. Even though I was sitting there staring at pictures of my birth father, Tess's comment suddenly lessened him to a faceless, stereotypical black man in America, and suddenly Dad, the only father I'd ever known, fell into the void created by Tess's racism.

I gathered the pictures up and put them in my bag to bring home to Warner, thinking that when I got home, I would ask Dad his feelings about black people, whether he'd had any black friends growing up, and maybe I'd show him the pictures of Joe Banks if he seemed interested.

"The blacks mostly kept to themselves," Dad said plainly, when I asked him if he'd ever had any black friends. "But I was mostly interested in girls, and turtles, of course."

"But there were black students at your school in Groton, right?" Dad had gone to a public high school in Groton, Connecticut, which, he'd told me before, was integrated with black students.

"Yes, a handful," he said. "But like I said, they really just pre-ferred to keep to themselves."

"Did you ever think that might be about self-preservation in a predominantly white environment?"

"I never really thought about it, Beck," Dad said.

"Did you think about trying to make friends with any of them?"

"They weren't interested in being friends with white people."

"And since then, though," I said, struggling to map this out in my brain, "no black friends. You and Mom have never had black friends."

"Well, look around, Beck!" Dad laughed, thinking the whiteness of our town and immediate surroundings was funny.

"That's kind of my point, Dad. Look around!"

"Of course there was my friend Lee Ling, when I was at the Museum School," Dad offered. "And he was just a great friend, and all."

"Also Chinese."

"Yes, Lee Ling was this little Chinese guy, funny as hell," Dad said. "I don't know, Beck. I've mostly chosen to live in places where there aren't that many humans in general, I really need to be around the natural world."

"But didn't you think it might be important if you were raising a black child for her to see other black people?"

"Mom and I both really thought the world was changing, and that people were coming toward each other," Dad said. "We really believed what Martin Luther King was saying. And, you know, we had those wonderful years on the Hill together and all. And this beautiful house we have now. I mean, how lucky are we?"

I didn't show the two pictures I had of my birth father to Dad. Instead, I kept them, and him, and us, to ourselves. Like the black kids he'd described in his high school.

Twenty-Two

I had started working any job I could as soon as I was hireable, because I wanted things, and Mom and Dad couldn't afford to buy them for me. I liked nice clothes and shoes and bags and jewelry—Tess said I was too materialistic—and so I had to make my own money in order to get them.

When I was seventeen, I worked at a local oil company, a small and disorganized office. Everything felt shoved into the one room, with two chairs for customers waiting for service; a front desk, where I sat; a smaller desk behind me, where Joyce the accountant sat; and a tiny bathroom squeezed in between both our desks, but closer to Joyce's. Dennis, who was my boss and also the guy in the family who drove the oil truck, was probably 250 pounds of anger and bitterness. He liked to demean me in front of customers, or just Joyce if there were no customers waiting, which was often the case. "Yuh think yuh so smaht, goin' off to college. Yuh ain't that smaht. Yuh workin' here, ain't-cha?"

Dennis often asked me to do things that weren't actually part of my job. "Run up the staw-uh, get me a sandwich." This time it was cleaning the bathroom. We actually had a cleaning person who came in to clean the office during the weekends, but that day, after Dennis came in from a delivery and took a humongous dump in the toilet, he decided that he wanted me to clean the bathroom.

He left the door open after so that we could smell it, looked at me, and said, "Clean it up."

Joyce, a chatty twenty-something whose life revolved around her job, Weight Watchers, and her boyfriend, just sat there, pretending she was adding something up on her desk calculator. "I am the secretary, not the cleaning lady," I said. Dennis stood at the corner of my desk, reeking of oil and shit, his brown uniform disheveled, gut hanging out over his belt. "Lazy nigger," he scoffed, and walked out the door.

The bells on the door of the oil company, intended to announce a customer's arrival, didn't so much ring as crash against the door when Dennis slammed it shut behind him. I looked behind me at Joyce, who kept her head down and punched numbers into her desktop accountant's calculator. "Did you hear that?"

Joyce said nothing.

I stood up from my desk and walked out of the office, up the hill to the local grocery "staw-uh," and applied for a job as a cashier. A couple weeks later, Joyce came through my line. She bought a 3 Musketeers bar and a Coke, giving me a meek smile as she paid, before whispering, "Good for you."

Perched on the lip of the tub that night, I looked at myself, hair still in a cropped afro, the style I'd kept since Tess took me to the fancy 210 hair salon two years before. And then I started to have a conversation with myself.

"I mean, these are the *people*," I said to my reflection, affecting the tone of a commentator or talk show host, "who are out here, owning local businesses, who are responsible for the town's economy. What do you make of it, Rebecca?"

I was less Oprah, whom I loved and rushed home to watch at four p.m. every afternoon before I started working after school, even though her audiences were always overwhelmingly white back then, and more like Phil Donahue, whose *Donahue Show* I also watched religiously.

I shifted my posture, picked my head back up, looked straight at my reflection. "Honestly, I wish I knew. I would say that he's probably quite pathetic," I said, trying to come across as both indifferent and brilliant, in jeans and a T-shirt with the face of China Girl from David Bowie's video for the song on the front.

"And are you sure you heard what you think you heard? He used *that* word?" I questioned myself.

"Yes, I am. I mean, how do you mistake that word for any other?" I responded, unable to say it out loud myself.

When it came time for college, no one was less interested than my parents, which Tess found utterly unacceptable. As far as she was concerned, I was *going* to college. "I haven't worked this hard on you for this long for you to just throw it away, Rebecca," she said.

I likely would not have gone without her insistence.

Neither Riana nor Sean went to college, which Tess posited was a Machiavellian tactic on Dad's part, a way to elevate his star child, me, as a peer, while keeping his biological children lowbrow and in awe of his genius. I wasn't ready to decide whether I agreed with her assessment, but I had certainly begun to question how Riana and Sean had veered so wildly from the direction of books and art.

Sean married young at twenty, like Mom and Dad had, to an older woman with a six-year-old daughter from a previous marriage. He found steady work as a carpenter, welcomed a son, and built a gigantic house on the top of a small knoll for his new family just outside of Warner that featured turtle tanks and aquariums, a live, rooted tree that grew up through the living room floor, and a screened-in porch, all reminiscent of our first house on Pumpkin

Hill. Sean had also taken charge of upkeep on our house, often in need of repair.

Sean's wife, Mary, was intense, capable, and direct, and she made Sean happy as the day was long. My brother and I had nothing in common whatsoever, but I was very glad for his happiness, glad to share a beer with him when I was home, even though I hated beer. Glad to go out in a fishing boat with him on the pond or lake near Warner in an attempt to bond, although I hated fishing almost as much as I hated beer, and he never asked me questions about my life or college or what I was interested in.

Riana married one in her string of abusive boyfriends she'd started seeing when she was a teenager, and moved to northern New Hampshire, where she worked as a prep cook at a place called the Buck Rub Pub. She also gave birth to twin boys born with a rare neuromuscular disorder called multicore, an aggressive disease that causes a lack of muscle tissue, delayed motor skills, and curvature of the spine inward toward the chest cavity, and results in respiratory issues.

The initial diagnosis for the boys was that they would never walk on their own, and likely wouldn't live past ten. It was touch and go for a few days after they were born, and I remember being home with Mom and Dad at the end of the summer before my senior year, waiting by the phone to find out if they would be all right, worried about Riana, thinking about how sweet and silly she'd been when we were kids, how wild and radiant her laughter had been. And then, after that night, how she had become someone else, and dropped out of high school for several months before ultimately returning to graduate.

I was a decent student, but not a great one. I did well in English, literature, and writing, but failed repeatedly in math and science.

My PSAT and SAT scores were abysmal, which the guidance counselor at Kearsarge told me would limit my options considerably. "Maybe consider a community college," he suggested. Meanwhile, all of my friends were applying to Dartmouth and Wesleyan and Bates and Middlebury—all of New England's finest liberal arts schools.

"You could probably get into Dartmouth just based on, you know, being black," Nate said one day when we were talking about colleges in the school resource center. "I mean, that's like a thing."

In retrospect I think of how appealing I would have been to the admissions board if I'd written about how my friend, a popular white boy who bought me as his slave in middle school, and whose racist father taught social studies at our high school, had then suggested I take advantage of the practice or policy of favoring groups of folks who have been discriminated against based on their skin color. Now *that* would have been a college essay.

In truth, I don't remember what I ended up writing my college essay on, though almost certainly it had to do with getting out of Warner. Frankly, I wasn't that enthused about college at all. I still aspired to become an actor, even though I did only one play in high school, because theater in high school was for theater geeks, not the popular crew I ran with. And despite Tess's condemnation of acting as a career pursuit, I applied to NYU's Tisch School of the Arts, among half a dozen other schools that didn't appeal much.

Weeks later, when all the applications were in, I sat on the toilet seat in the bathroom upstairs next to my room, and talked with the Tisch School dean of admissions about my chances in an informal interview. He was impressed with my writing, but feared the financial aid offerings might be too bleak. "New York is *very* expensive," he said with a patronizing chuckle.

✦ ✦

I did not want to go to the University of New Hampshire, less than a hundred miles away in Durham. I wanted to get out of New Hampshire, and move to New York. And I wanted to be around black people. But nobody asked me about that, and I didn't know to ask anyone. Nobody suggested an HBCU (Historically Black Colleges and Universities), something I'd never even heard of, or asked how I felt about seventeen years in a small rural town, engulfed by whiteness, quietly amassing and internalizing moments of targeted racism.

We held my high school graduation party on the patch of green grass in front of the first of two gardens behind the house. Tess, who drove from Portsmouth with the boys, sat on the ground casually, legs crossed, with Sebastian in her lap and Mateo hanging over her shoulder, relaxed and carefree with the children she kept attached to her body, while Mom hustled about making sure everyone had food and drinks, taking pictures and making conversation.

A handful of friends from school came, along with my brother and his family, but not my sister, who lived too far away. Leah was still away at private school, and Dad didn't come either; he had other things to do that day. It was an informal gathering hastily thrown together by me the week before, when I'd decided I wanted to feel celebrated for making it through high school in one piece. But now it felt ill-thought-out and weirdly disjointed, as my French teacher, whom I loved, tried to make small talk with my brother, and everyone pretended it was completely normal for my adoptive mother and my birth mother to just be hanging out together.

In reality, it was the first time that Mom and Tess had been in the same space for any length of time, or together in a social setting at all, and as I watched Mom rush around in her pretty floral dress and black pumps, all smiles, hosting the party with everything she had, while Tess sat relaxing on the grass, literally wearing her young children, I suddenly felt gutted. I felt sorry for Mom, and envious of my brothers. Then I felt ashamed for pitying Mom, and for wishing Tess had kept me so that I could be one of her young kids curled up in her lap, hanging on her shoulder, skin to skin with the same body we were born out of.

I moved from friend to friend, trying to feel celebratory, but instead feeling caught in the crosshairs of where unconditional love met conditional love. It was like being simultaneously owned and disowned—pushed over an edge and scooped up just before hitting the ground.

✢ Twenty-Three ✢

A couple of months later, I arrived in Durham, a town that, despite having spent most of three summers adjacent to it, I knew little to nothing about. There was a main strip where all the frats were, known as Frat Row, where boys would hold up score cards when girls walked by, a large books and supply store, a diner, a bagel shop, and a CVS. Two big twin dorms that stretched toward the sky were set back from town, on the far end of campus. I was assigned one of those dorms, which I hated on sight. I counted four black people on registration day.

Girls on my floor with frosted hair and blue eye shadow spoke with loud New Hampshire and Massachusetts accents, wearing their acid-wash jeans tucked into their little white socks.

The one bright spot at UNH was Sarah. She was a friend from childhood, an upbeat, whip-smart beauty who had moved away in middle school, and showed up at UNH begrudgingly, like me. Sarah also had been relegated to our state university for financial reasons, and as a dual citizen of France and the United States who spoke three languages and had seen the entire world over, she found UNH as glaringly provincial and limited as I did. We ended up in the same dorm together, and picked things up where we'd left off in middle school. Sarah was not preppy or moneyed; she was cultured and self-aware, raised with a black stepmother who was from Guadeloupe.

If the first semester at UNH was miserable, the second semester was a marked improvement. I applied and was accepted to move into Smith, the dorm for international students, which wasn't limited to international students, and was really more a safe house for folks who might be perceived as other. As such, it was the most diverse space on campus, and soon after I moved in, I lobbied for Sarah to get a spot as well—Sarah, who was, at least by half, actually an international student.

We roomed together on the top floor of Smith's four stories, and plastered our walls with posters of David Bowie (Sarah's long-time obsession), shared clothes, and laughed a lot. It was a balm for me, but also an opportunity to establish a healthy, compatible friendship with someone who had traveled the world, whose perspective was global, far beyond the confines of lily-white New Hampshire.

Sarah studied international politics, while I shifted toward literature after trying and failing to keep up in the university's esteemed politics program Sarah was enrolled in during the first semester. The idea of politics appealed to me partly because it seemed like a sophisticated thing to know about, to be learned in, but mainly because I didn't know what else to study at a place that felt so insanely banal.

I also had started writing for the school's newspaper and magazine, at Tess's encouragement, and discovered I liked it.

I leaned heavily into the proximity to Tess and my brothers in that first year, frequently joining them for dinner and borrowing Tess's car to get back to campus. After one dinner late in the first semester, the night before finals, we'd just put the boys to bed, and I was getting ready to leave. "Drive carefully," Tess said. "I mean it."

I promised that I would. The snow had already started as I pulled out of the parking lot of her housing tenement where she lived with the boys. It was dark and hard to see, but I drove slowly along with the few other cars on the stretch of Route 4 between Portsmouth and Durham. I kept my eye on the speedometer, because I knew that if anything happened and it was discovered that I had been driving too fast, Tess would be livid.

Mine was the only car on the road when I hit a patch of ice. The wheel turned abruptly to the right, and the car swerved uncontrollably. I panicked and turned the wheel the other way, exactly what you're not supposed to do.

I got out of the car and saw that I'd hit a telephone pole. The right headlight was smashed, and there was a considerable dent in the fender. It was snowing hard now, and absolutely freezing. There were no cell phones. No one else was on the road. I wasn't physically hurt, but I was terrified and shaken. Not as much terrified to be alone on the side of the road in the middle of the night on a dark snowy night as I was in anticipation of how Tess was going to respond to the accident. I walked to the nearest house, which luckily was not too far, and asked to use the phone to call a tow truck. The tow truck driver gave me a ride back to my dorm, and I called Tess from the pay phone on our floor.

"How bad is the damage to the car?" she asked. I'd known she would be angry, but I wasn't ready for the callousness in her voice. "You're going to have to pay for it yourself, you know." Tears streamed down my face. I nodded over the phone as if she could hear the gesture. "You understand?" I managed to get a yes out before hanging up the phone.

I deposited more coins into the slot and dialed home. "Mom,

I was in an accident with Tess's car." Before I could say another word, Mom said, in a panic, "My God, are you all right?" I slid down the wall next to the phone, my back pressed and tight, eyes closed and wet. "I'm OK, Mom."

I sobbed in my bed for the rest of the night, soaking my pillow all the way through. Sarah tried to comfort and console me, but there was nothing. I couldn't even articulate why I was crying so hard. It was beyond my control. It was compulsive. It felt deadly. I couldn't get away from it. That was the night that I learned the difference between my mom and my birth mother. The precise and harrowing elucidation of unconditional love versus conditional love that I'd felt at my high school graduation party, but had been unable to articulate.

Twenty-Four

An essay I wrote for the UNH magazine that took aim at the school's lack of diversity, and how the demographics, while firmly reflective of the state of New Hampshire's, should be more inclusive, led to a few public speaking engagements, and also granted me an invitation by the UNH President's Commission on the Status of Women to attend a private luncheon with Angela Davis. I couldn't take my eyes off her, sitting at the head of a long table set with plates of fruit and pastries.

She wore dreadlocks then, a hairstyle that I didn't understand, and had grown up judging as dirty, matted hair. I knew people made a choice to wear their hair that way, but I didn't understand why they would want to. *Who wants to run their fingers through that?* I had learned from Tess that one of the most appealing and sought-after things about a woman for a man was the idea of running his fingers through her hair.

Seeing Angela's dreadlocks changed my entire way of thinking: they didn't wear her, she wore them, and they seemed simultaneously ancient and modern. She looked like a goddess to me, and her voice, majestic and commanding, sounded like unapologetic power. I began to think about organizing around my blackness, and the celebration of black culture, for the first time.

I asked around, and after learning that there hadn't been a

Black Student Union on campus in twenty years, I decided to start it back up. Starting a Black Student Union and actually running it were, of course, two different things, and I had no idea where to begin.

And then I met Elijah Freeman.

Classes with Elijah were legendary at UNH, where he'd been teaching black literature and writing as the university's only black male professor for nearly twenty years. He was a fiercely committed and charismatic teacher. Tall and lithe with a graying afro and tawny brown skin, Elijah was stern but engaged. He loved what he did and it showed.

"Oh, yeah, Elijah," Tess said when I told her that I'd signed up for his class. "I had him when I was at UNH."

How had Tess not mentioned that she'd had such a well-regarded black professor as a student there when she was trying to convince me that UNH was my best bet? He was a beacon for the few black students on campus, and a high-profile veteran of the university, not just as a professor but also as a black man navigating white spaces.

"Why didn't you mention him before?" I asked at the kitchen table in Tess's apartment.

"Because he has major women issues, like, *major*. He, like, *wicked* can't deal with women." Her response was so flip that it immediately seemed suspicious.

I was still stinging a bit from the car accident, and Tess's attendant reproach. I wasn't in the mood. "Well, I guess we'll just have to see," I said. Tess shrugged her shoulders and left the room.

I sat in the front row for every class, and soaked in Elijah's words and wisdom like gospel. He commanded the classroom as he spoke about James Baldwin and Toni Morrison, whose novel *Sula* became my bible after I first read it in his class. He talked about the power of words and how integral history, all history, but especially black history, is to the way that we use language, the way we write about ourselves and the world around us. How we think about history as we write, he said, is what turns an essay into literature. I wrote about books by Alice Walker, Gwendolyn Brooks, Nella Larsen, and Toni Cade Bambara.

Their words and worlds, and the structure and grace across every page, felt biblical and made my insides churn and my mind explode. It was like guzzling love, fast and warm and sweet in my throat. Thousands of words would present themselves, breathe and carry ideas and images clear through to the very end of an entire book without mentioning a white character.

Zora Neale Hurston's essay "How It Feels to Be Colored Me" resonated so deeply with me I could hardly believe it. I felt rage that I was only discovering her so long after I'd needed her, which was from the beginning. *Sometimes, I feel discriminated against, but it does not make me angry*, Hurston wrote. *It merely astonishes me. How can any deny themselves the pleasure of my company? It's beyond me.*

I used that quote as the starting point, and wrote an essay I didn't know I could write about how I managed to navigate my high school experience without falling into despair—how somewhere deep down, I always believed my company was worthwhile, despite the rejection and the racism, and that maybe, just maybe, the white boys who didn't like me "that way," and my racist teachers and racist boss at the oil company, were missing out on something lovely. They were missing out on me.

You're gaining steam! Elijah wrote in his comments.

I wasn't a great writer right away, but I wrote well in high school, and stronger than I ever had before in Elijah's class, and his

encouragement and advice on how and where I could improve—
Remove the ego from your work or *Is this really what you're trying to say?*
Go deeper—made me more confident with what I could aim for.

When I shared my essays from class with Tess, she brought out
the writing she'd done when she had taken the same class, work
she'd saved for unknown reasons that I didn't ask about. "Feel free
to use these as guidance," she said, laying a folder of single-spaced,
one-page essays, with her name typed at the top, dated from 1971
or thereabouts, with the same black scratch of Elijah's handwriting in the margins. *Make your point more clear*, one read. *This seems
harsh*, said another.

After my first class with Elijah, and changing my major from
political science to English, I decided to request him as my primary academic advisor. In our first official meeting as advisor and
advisee, I asked him about Tess. "Do you remember a student in
the '70s named Tess Bancroft?"

He raised his eyebrows and cocked his head slightly. "Ah, yes.
Why?"

"Well, she's my birth mother, and we're pretty close, and she
told me that you were her teacher, too, and that you hate women."
I didn't plan to say any of this, but it's what came out all at once
before I'd had a chance to think.

Elijah just stared at me for a minute, somber and still, weighing
his words.

I plowed on, filling the awkward silence. "I mean, it's a very
difficult relationship, as you can imagine," I continued, thoughts
just tumbling out uncontrollably now. I'd never talked to anyone
so openly about Tess before. And that I was talking so openly about
her to my first adult black male role model felt like a release, like
opening floodgates I hadn't even known existed. "And I'm actually

feeling really unsure, or, I don't know, like there's something not right about it, and I'm just, I guess, really confused."

Elijah crossed his legs and rested both of his hands, one on top of the other, on his knee. His office was a windowless room, but somehow always felt filled with the kind of warmth only the sun creates. Shelves lined with books, stacks of papers to be graded on his desk. "What I remember about Tess is that she was very smart, very stubborn, and that she had some issues with black folks," he finally said.

"Issues with black folks? How? What do you mean?" I sat on the edge of the smooth leather couch in his office opposite his desk, and then, feeling too eager, leaned back and folded my arms across my chest to try to look cooler. Elijah said he thought she was too smug about black culture, as if she knew everything there was to know about black folks, and had trouble deferring to the experience of actual black people. I heard this as him letting me in on something, sharing authentic black knowledge that I couldn't get anywhere else, especially not from Tess.

"I feel so torn," I confided. And I did. For the first time, someone, another black person, an adult black person, was articulating what I had been feeling about Tess for years regarding race. "It's just so weird, right? She slips into what she thinks is a black woman's voice, or makes all these authoritative statements about black boys and men, like, why?"

That, Elijah said, is what racism is, and how racism works. It gives white people the power to interpret or outright co-opt our experiences, our voices and identities, as they like, whenever they like. "Look, I have no animosity toward Tess, but to be perfectly honest, I'm worried about you," Elijah said. "I don't believe she deserves your loyalty."

I needed someone to say this. Someone to look out for me, to recognize the damage she was doing to my self-esteem, to notice the way I second-guessed myself whenever I brought her name up. How my body language changed, and the tenor of my voice ripped through my chest, in turns strident and shaken.

I gave another talk at UNH about my own personal experience growing up in rural New Hampshire, trying to navigate my blackness, feeling isolated and either unseen or overseen. I emphasized how difficult and disheartening it was to be at a school that so vividly reflected that experience, and how necessary it was for the few black students at UNH to feel empowered.

Tess was in the audience, and afterward we went for coffee at a diner on campus.

"You seemed uncomfortable up there at times," Tess said.

"I was nervous," I said defensively. It was only my second time giving a public speech to such a large audience.

"It felt to me like you were playing at being black," she said. "Like you didn't really know how to embody your sense of self as a black woman." I could feel her eyes boring into me, swimming around under my skin with sharp, tiny fins.

"I've learned a lot in Elijah's class, just from writing and reading, listening to him talk about black culture and history," I said.

"Taking a class with a black professor doesn't make you black, Rebecca," Tess said dismissively.

"Shouldn't I get to decide what makes me black?" I said, feeling agitated, under attack, bullied—as if even the most truthful explanation of how I was feeling came across desperate.

"But how would you know, Rebecca?" Tess said this as if it were the eighteen thousandth time she'd had to articulate this to me. "I've been around far more black people than you have—culture is more than skin color, and Elijah is obviously trying to take advantage of your naivete."

"But why?"

"For his ego, Rebecca! What do you think?"

A few weeks later, Tess announced she would be starting in the master's program at UNH in the fall. Couldn't she just let me have this one experience? Had she planned all along to come back to UNH? Was she doing it so that she could keep an eye on me and Elijah?

Luckily, I was already planning to transfer out of UNH. I learned about a school called Hampshire College through the dean of minorities at Brown University, where I'd first set my sights when I decided that I had to leave UNH. Again, the dean at Brown, like the dean at NYU, said the issue of money would be a stumbling block, and asked if I'd heard of this school Hampshire. He said it had a reputation for being a bit of a hippie school, but that it was making a concerted effort at diversifying its student body, and its curriculum, self-designed, seemed like it might be right for me based on the conversations we had.

I scheduled an interview at Hampshire, and was, to my surprise, met by a black woman, Sunny, an assistant dean of students, who gave me a tour. She was very candid about the school's lack of diversity, but also said she was encouraged by Hampshire's rigorous diversity initiatives. We strolled through campus, a lateral, village-like compound with utilitarian structures, nothing especially pretty or bucolic like UNH's campus, which immediately and ironically put me at ease. I'd had enough bucolic to last me a lifetime. Sunny said there was a strong, if small, community of color that was inclusive and low-key.

Students we passed on their way to and from classes looked both focused and relaxed, as if they were walking in a direction they wanted to go. Sunny told me about Hampshire's membership in the Five College Consortium; how, as a Hampshire student, I would be able to take classes at one of the other colleges—Smith, Mount Holyoke, Amherst, and UMass Amherst—which offered a nice way to get off campus, which could start to feel insular after a while.

"But tell the truth," I said. "Do you feel like the only one? Like the only black person in the room, like all the time?"

Sunny stopped, gave me a knowing smile. "I wouldn't be here if I did."

Sunny's close-cut afro suited her round, inviting face. She was both honest and critical as she explained that more and more black students were coming in every year, and that black students from the other colleges frequently took classes at Hampshire, widely viewed as the most experimental and challenging of the five schools. Sunny also pointed out that, while there were by no means enough, the school had black staff and professors, none of whom were shy about throwing down the gauntlet when it came to conversations about race and racism within the Hampshire community, and in the broader national discourse.

"We are, like most things, a work in progress," Sunny said. "But I promise you will not feel like the only one here, and you will be able to take control of your studies and direct your interests in a way that you can't really do anywhere else."

Convinced it would be a better environment for me, I applied to Hampshire, and was awarded a full academic scholarship. The fall semester at UNH would be my last.

Twenty-Five

I was waitressing at a resort hotel a few miles away from where Riana lived the summer after my first year at UNH. I'd found the job through the job board at UNH, and had heard that you could make big money at places like this. When Riana found out I was so close, she invited me over one afternoon. I borrowed a coworker's car and drove to her house, a small cabin cowering under a scant grouping of trees, with a vacant dirt driveway.

The house's interior—the laundry piled up on the couch, formula canisters and baby bottles half full on the kitchen counter, garbage spilling over and out of its container, small harnesses to carry bodies that couldn't crawl or move properly on their own—reflected the life of a single working mother overwhelmed by twin babies with health issues. Even though Riana technically was not single, she might as well have been. Her husband, Eddie, who I knew had beaten her more than once, was of little to no help with the boys, resented their disease, and blamed Riana for it.

Sun crept uneasily through the dirty panes of two windows as the babies now started to coo, the sound coming as a relief, and the smell of something rotten rose up every now and then. It was my day off, and I suddenly wished I was spending it in a more pleasant way. Riana moved things around, pushed a few blankets to the side of the couch so that I could sit.

"You want anything to drink, Becca? Coffee?" Riana asked. She was the only one in our family who called me Becca, and she always said it in a soft, plucky tone.

"I'm good," I said, feeling uncomfortable about feeling so uncomfortable.

Riana had always been naturally thin, but now she was downright gaunt, maybe ninety pounds at just five feet tall, less than a year after giving birth to twins. She still wore her hair in the same style as when we were kids, in banana curls around her face like Farrah Fawcett. Her eyes were bloodshot and her skin weathered, a front tooth chipped from when she'd fallen, drunk at a party in high school, that had never been fixed or replaced. She still smoked a pack of cigarettes a day, but tried not to smoke directly around the babies.

"I just wanted to see the horses," she started while my nephews lay on the floor in just diapers, unsettlingly quiet, arms and legs splayed, limp. Riana then told me for the first time what had happened that night ten years before, when she'd pushed past me through the bathroom, into our bedroom, as the fumes of her anger trailed behind her like the dust tail of a comet. She told me she was raped at a county fair that night by boys who had lured her into the dark with the promise of showing her their prizewinning horses.

"But why didn't you tell the police?" I asked, knowing nothing then about how seldom women are believed when they report rape and sexual assault.

"I did," Riana told me. "After Mom and Dad came to get me, we went to the police station. And you know what happened? Their first question was, 'What were you wearing?' So I just left."

The memory of her pushing past me that night when we were

kids flashed before me. I felt so stupid, so judgmental, and so heart-broken for my sister. I also felt guilty: that I wasn't there for her. I had been too distracted, newly immersed in my reunion with Tess, my new brothers, and that world in Portsmouth. I didn't want Riana's messy pain, her dark and frightening defiance. I wanted my sister, the one who used to play horses with me, who had been so gentle and cheerful when we were kids. Not the girl who started to shout in my face when I told her to stop wearing my clothes. Not the girl who pushed me up against the wall and tried to leach her anger into the peeling paint behind my head.

But I could be here for her now. At this moment. I got up to hug her—her hair smelled of cigarettes and the shampoo from our teen years, Fabergé Organics with Wheat Germ Oil and Honey in the orange bottle with the peach-colored cap.

"I'm so sorry, Riana," I said. It was not nearly enough. "And it's bullshit that Mom and Dad didn't do anything about it, or take you to talk to someone, or something."

She shrugged, the tears in her eyes giving way to that radiant, goofy smile of hers from when we were kids.

"Love you," she said, as she always did when we parted or got off the phone with each other, as rare as our visits and phone conversations had become, with a kind of vulnerable stoicism in her voice, a genuine hope that our bond would return to the days when we played her game of horses in the living room of the house on the hill.

In the same way I was only able to understand my parents' "open marriage" through popular culture references, when Riana told me about her rape, all I could think of was *The Burning Bed*, the TV movie starring Farrah Fawcett, Riana's hair doppelganger, based on the same-titled book, about a woman who lives with her viciously abusive husband until one night, after he falls asleep, she sets his bed on fire. I wanted Riana to find that same courage and rage, if not necessarily to burn her boyfriend to death while he was sleeping, but to stop taking the abuse. Riana was a fighter, but she was also hell-bent on being hurt, surrendering herself over to a violence she felt she deserved.

Mom and Dad, generally hands-off as parents to begin with, now viewed Riana as an adult who should make her own decisions about relationships.

I wish I could say that this visit with my only sister, when she told me the story of her rape at fourteen, brought us closer, or back together, but it didn't. I was going back to college soon, and she was going to stay in her marriage to Eddie, an abusive man, while trying to manage the special needs of her children, all in a remote town at the northern tip of New Hampshire, where the pipes froze in winter and the air conditioner was too expensive to leave on in the summer.

A few weeks later I was at home and confronted Mom about the rape, and why they didn't do anything.

"We tried, *I* tried, to get her to talk to someone after it happened," Mom explained. "But she wouldn't go. She refused, and we couldn't force her."

I could hear Mom's maternal instincts flare as I pushed her.

"She didn't want to talk anymore to the police, who were really just terrible to her," Mom said, her voice fluttering with worry and an underlying incredulity, the way it did when she realized, or had decided, that there was nothing she could do about a bad situation.

"I truly do not understand why you didn't insist," I said. "It's insane to me."

"Well, Beck," Mom said, getting flustered, "you just can't make people do things they don't want to do is all." And I knew that was the end of the conversation. Why was I the only one in the family who found this unacceptable? Why was it a secret, which could only serve to make Riana feel more shame around it? Why didn't Mom and Dad want to file charges against these boys who sexually violated their fourteen-year-old daughter? Did Sean know? Why didn't *he* want to make sure these boys were caught and punished? Then, of course, I had to turn the questioning inward: Why didn't *I* take this on and seek out justice for my sister?

✢ Twenty-Six ✢

The plan was for me to finish the fall semester at UNH, hand off the leadership duties of my fledgling Black Student Union to a more seasoned student organizer, and then take the spring and summer off before transferring to Hampshire. My high school friend, also named Rebecca who went by the nickname Beck, and I were going to leave in February to drive across the country and settle in California for the summer. I was so very ready to get away from UNH.

The Memorial Union Building, or the MUB, was right in the center of campus. I was there frequently to put up flyers about the Black Student Union, or to meet with fellow organizers from other affinity groups. It was the main hub for all student life and activities, where you could leave mail for teachers, switch classes, or file for a transcript. I was just walking out after posting about an upcoming meeting when Elijah walked in, and we paused for a moment to talk. He told me how proud of me he was for the success of the BSU, which was modest but alive, and what a powerful mark I'd made and the legacy I was leaving. I thanked him for the kind words and for being an important figure for me at a critical time in my life.

"Well, look who's here," Elijah said, looking past my shoulders.

I turned to see Tess heading straight into the main office without seeing us.

"Great," I said, with mock sarcasm.

"She's looking a little broad in the hips these days," Elijah said casually.

"Yeah, I guess," I said, taken entirely off guard. I wasn't even sure I'd heard him correctly. But as soon as I said it, I immediately felt sick, and everything and everyone around me became a blur. I'd never heard Elijah say anything so crass about Tess. He'd questioned my loyalty to her, which I also openly questioned with him, and taken aim at her character, but never at her physical appearance.

"OK, gotta go," I said, agitated. "I really don't want to deal with her right now anyway, so I'll talk to you later." I turned to leave without saying goodbye.

I struggled with whether to tell Tess what he'd said, torn between my gratitude toward Elijah, who had saved my life at UNH, and my loyalty to Tess, whose approval somehow still defined me. But I knew what he'd said was wrong, and about a week later I decided to drive out to Portsmouth to tell her in person.

"I told you, he truly hates women," she said. "Let's take him down. Ruin him. Just you and me together."

It seemed like the silver bullet she'd been waiting for—from the first time I'd mentioned his name to her, she never wasted an opportunity to express her disdain for him. Meanwhile, I felt like my body was spilling, parts from the inside pouring out from under my fingernails and through the roots of my hair. Elijah was the first black father figure I'd ever had, and it was devastating to think I was about to lose that. But it seemed like I had no choice.

Tess proposed that we craft a letter to Elijah laying out in detail how he'd failed me as a professor and advisor, and been egregiously malicious toward Tess. "We can write it together," she said. But what she really meant was that she would essentially write it, and I would sign it as if it had been written by me, which is exactly what happened. I believed that she was doing this for me, for us, as a way to reignite and strengthen our bond, which had been slowly coming apart since the car accident during my first semester a year before.

Dear Elijah,

UNH has been grim. It has been intellectually bleak. There have been, however, moments to stay for . . . those moments have been primarily provided by you. Mentor is too strong a word, but certainly you have guided and inspired. And this is why I'm writing with regret and disappointment.

    I have been puzzled by your consistently mean-spirited comments about Tess, my mother. I am further baffled by why you feel free to do this. Sheer confusion has inhibited my expressing this to you. I'm nothing short of stunned at the shallowness of this. Surely you can understand the seriousness of mother/daughter relationships. If I have spoken ill of her, I did so in confidence and out of trust. It appears that this has come back at me venomously. Besides, I can say anything I want about her, she's my mother—that is my right. Moreover, I am bothered by what I perceive as the misuse of your power as my advisor. What can you hope to expect from belittling my mother to me? What is your intent?

    And finally, I feel robbed of a good reason to stay at UNH. Perhaps I have leaned on you too heavily, or hoped for too much from you, and for that I take full responsibility. It has been my perception that she has no animosity toward you, yet still—if you have an issue with her, take it up with her. Why am I involved? Am I a vent for your anger? I don't want to be a medium for that.

Rebecca

I left the letter in Elijah's department mailbox, feeling ill and fraudulent—he *was* my mentor, and I missed him already. Two days passed before I saw him again, this time as he was leaving the Humanities and Arts building and I was entering. It was raining, gray and bleak outside, and he held an umbrella overhead as he stood on the lower step to the building, stopping me before I could disappear inside.

"Was that really necessary?" Elijah said, his eyes glazed over. He looked so disappointed, so genuinely hurt. He shook his head. "You deserve better."

In less than twenty-four hours, Tess had called the dean, and she, Elijah, and I were in his office, with Tess and Elijah yelling back and forth at each other while I sat in between them, sobbing. Tess insisted Elijah be fired for abusing his power over me, while Elijah shot back that she was just using me as a pawn to vindicate the grudge she'd held against him for twenty years over some comments he'd made about her writing. The dean, a slender white man with glasses, sat across from the three of us, the letter in hand, eyebrows furrowed, utterly bewildered.

"Let's all cool down," he said. "Clearly Rebecca is very upset." He asked me if I wanted to say anything, and I shook my head, unable to speak, chest heaving. Then he asked if I wanted to file a complaint or something like that, and I shook my head again, no.

This would be the first of many traumas. My bond with Elijah would be the first of many major casualties that resulted from my relationship with Tess.

Twenty-Seven

At UNH, my American literature class started at nine a.m., and was about a ten-minute walk from my dorm. It was cold and slushy outside as I rushed across campus, trying to avoid puddles, my feet already freezing in beat-up Tretorn sneakers. I ran up the stairs of the English building and stopped short at the classroom door to readjust my energy level before quietly pushing the door open and taking a seat right inside.

"*The World According to Garp*," our professor said. "What does everyone think?"

I shot my hand up from my seat in the second row. It took my professor a minute to place me, since I always sat in the front row.

"Yes, Rebecca," she said. "Thoughts?"

"Asshole?" I said.

"Yes." She smiled. "Definitely an asshole. But do you mean T. S. Garp or John Irving?"

The entire class erupted into laughter, and one boy laughed a little longer, keeping his gaze on me.

I'd noticed Wyatt in class before, although he never said much. He was ridiculously good-looking, as if he'd stepped straight out of a J.Crew catalog, clean-cut with floppy, chestnut-brown hair and intense blue eyes. As class let out and everyone was gathering up their books, with our teacher telling us to have a good Christmas break, Wyatt approached me to ask if I had plans to go to some party on campus over the weekend.

Wyatt was slightly sheepish, but quietly charming. He told me the details for the party, and I told him I'd think about it. I didn't go, but the following week, we ran into each other at the MUB, where I'd just had a final meeting to go over notes about BSU details, membership, and status. "Hey, hi!" Wyatt said, with boyish enthusiasm, his hand raised to flag me down. "Oh, hey," I said, feeling free. Free of the leadership responsibilities of the Black Student Union, soon to be free of UNH, ready to leave Tess and Elijah and Durham and Frat Row and dumb, useless, white-as-hell UNH behind. "Want to talk for a minute?"

Wyatt and I sat at a round table downstairs in the MUB next to the café, the dark movie room flickering behind us, *When Harry Met Sally* projected on a small screen on the wall, empty soda cans and chip bags strewn on nearby cushioned chairs. Wyatt told me he was from New Jersey, but had plans to ski in Vermont over winter break. I told him I grew up in New Hampshire, and would be going home for the break.

"Maybe you could meet me there?" Wyatt had a real grin to him, not just any old smile but a wide, all-the-way-across-his-face, full-on, beaming grin.

I smiled back. "Maybe." Even though I didn't think that was likely. He asked for my number in New Hampshire, and I gave it to him.

Wyatt was like my very own Jake from *Sixteen Candles*, the beautiful, popular white boy who in the end realizes he loves the shy, introverted, and overlooked girl, Sam. Not that I was shy or introverted or even overlooked, but something about all those things had added up in my mind as being less valuable than other girls, and that's how I'd felt in high school.

When we spoke on the phone, Wyatt said he would come back to campus early if I would come back, too, and go out on a date with him. I agreed.

Despite the dramatic incident with Elijah, which I had tried to block out of my mind because I felt so guilty and disloyal and stuck between them both, Tess was still my home base in Portsmouth, and of course my brothers, then eight and nine, were still my brothers.

Tess had recently moved from the housing projects into a spacious apartment in town with her new boyfriend, William, a successful and wealthy children's author and illustrator. Twenty years her senior, William was tall, white, handsome, and kind. We were all on the couch watching TV when Wyatt arrived to pick me up for our date in a blue-and-green-striped turtleneck, khakis, and boat shoes. Seconds later, Mateo said, in the uncensored outburst of a child, "You're right, Beck! He looks just like a J.Crew model!" Wyatt took it in stride, laughed to ease the silence, and introduced himself to Mateo, and everyone else, like a gentleman.

I chose Café Petronella when Wyatt asked me where I wanted to go for dinner. It felt good to bring an attractive date to the same spot where I used to come with my friend Monique after scooping ice cream all day over the summer, drinking Amaretto sours at the bar, while the bartenders drooled over her and ignored me. After we ordered, Wyatt told me that he had an adopted sister—a black adopted sister—he wanted me to meet.

Wyatt's mother, Alice, small and thin with a sharp, pretty face, served us cold casserole at the kitchen table, not even trying to hide her ire that we'd arrived two hours later than she'd expected us to arrive. Wyatt and I sat across from each other in silence while she placed forks next to our plates without offering anything else, and then stood against the stove sipping a glass of wine while we ate.

When Wyatt's sister Sophie emerged in the kitchen from her room upstairs, I nearly gasped out loud; the sense of empathy I felt was so immediate and strong it hurt. Sophie was a big girl, what pre-body-positive language would have called overweight, which I immediately understood was what Wyatt had meant when he'd told me she didn't take care of herself. Her hair was straightened with a perm, ends dry and split, and she wore it just below her ears, with barrettes clipped on each side, forcing it to do what white-girl hair did. Sophie had bright eyes and a candescent smile, full and rich and self-possessed, but there was also a melancholy pall around her that I felt certain only another interracial adoptee would detect.

In my journal that night, I wrote about my impressions of Sophie:

She is exactly like I was—in amongst a family of siblings, but she isn't one. It's difficult to describe, but all I can say is that for me to see a black girlchild in a white family moved me so much. She is totally solo—it's not like her siblings, who are biological siblings to each other, don't love her and she them, it's just different. She can't even pretend to be a genetic sib and that's tough.

There's that joke in big families where there's always the one kid who everyone else says "Where did mom find you?" Well that's real for me and Sophie. We came from somewhere else. Wyatt is very tight with his other siblings, and he loves Sophie, but there's something off. Just like me and Sean. It's no one's fault. It's like she's a well-respected guest, or good friend of the family. Or when you are talking with her, you need to be careful of what you say, be sure not to hurt her feelings or make her feel inferior, and then be sure she knows that's what they're doing on her behalf.

Sophie and I exchanged letters back and forth for months. She shared difficult, painful truths about feeling left out in the family, being discriminated against at school and her family's country club, where she knew she was only allowed in because her white family had a membership, her longing to be around other black people, what it meant to be "biracial," and not knowing how to talk to her mom about these things.

Sophie wrote to me about another thing that she said was especially hard to share, since she knew how much I loved Wyatt, and she loved him, too, but she needed to get it off her chest. She told me that Wyatt and their brother, Paul, had been cruel to her when she was a little girl, had made fun of her weight, poked and ridiculed her until she cried. This was alarming enough to me that I brought it up with Wyatt, who appeared palpably relieved, as if he'd been waiting to be able to talk about it with someone all these years. Wyatt told me, his eyes brimming with tears, that when he was old enough to realize what he and Paul had done to Sophie, he'd felt sick with regret, and still felt ashamed by his behavior.

Wyatt explained that he and Paul didn't know how to accept Sophie, that she was not only black but overweight as well, unlike his mother and sister and other white girls around them, who were all taut and slender, signaling discipline, commanding envy. Wyatt and Paul had both racially and morally judged Sophie, who, before me, had been on her own in navigating her racial identity. "I'm so glad she finally has someone to talk to," Wyatt said.

To hear this articulated, out loud, by a white boy who looked like he could have run with Nate and Ryan and Connor from high school was oddly gratifying. Wyatt didn't know how to talk about race, or his sister's experience and the ways in which she'd suffered because of it, but he trusted me enough to be honest and speak freely with me, his black girlfriend, about it.

Sophie wrote that more recently, Paul had suggested she "divorce" herself from being black. I was learning my own advice as I was giving it to her, but I wrote back to Sophie and told her that I disagreed with Paul, and that just because she wasn't raised to "act" black didn't mean she wasn't black. I wrote, *Actions come from upbringing, as well as soul.* I also told her that she could take control of her identity, own it however she wanted to, and that maybe she didn't have to run that by anybody in her family first.

I got things wrong in my advice to Sophie, too. I echoed the phrase Tess had assigned to me, "culturally white and cosmetically black," more than once, inadvertently pushing a mixed message about Sophie's identity. I tried to help her understand why the few other black kids at her school made fun of her and questioned the authenticity of her blackness, presuming to know what kids raised in black families think. *Inevitably culturally black kids are going to pass judgment on your "white lingo," but the reason why you don't know what you did to deserve their discrimination, is because you didn't do anything*, I wrote. *Black kids are uncomfortable that you and I look like them, but don't act like them, and from there it's easy for them to justify meanness and denying your roots. You are you. And you are not at fault.*

I never told her what Wyatt said about the cruelty, but I encouraged him to speak with her directly, to apologize and work it through. I don't know that he ever did.

✤ Twenty-Eight ✤

M_y *friend Beck and I had* been splitting driving shifts across the country, and with Beck sleeping next to me in the passenger seat, I cut my wee hours of the morning shift short because I thought I might fall asleep myself. I pulled off the road next to a sprawling cornfield to take a nap. We were off Route 40 somewhere in Kansas or Missouri, and just as I drifted off, Beck nearly bounded awake.

"Seriously? Are you kidding? What if someone's out here and attacks us?"

"Damn, Beck. Jesus, this isn't *Children of the Corn*. What are you worried about?" I said, trying to make light of the situation.

"Beck, we just came up from the South, where you ducked down in the passenger seat when we drove through a couple of towns. I'm just trying to keep us safe," Beck said.

It had somehow felt obvious to me to duck down unseen in the rural South, but now, as we drifted into the Midwest, it seemed more like New Hampshire, the home where I was raised, so I could feel safe taking a nap in a car pulled over on the shoulder of an untraveled road.

Driving shifts and danger zones aside, I knew the minute Beck and I got on the road that there was no way in hell I was sticking with our original plan of staying in San Francisco for the summer.

Wyatt and I talked on the phone at every stop along the way, and he flew out to meet us in Santa Fe, New Mexico, during his spring break in March, when we were just a few weeks into the trip.

One night when he was with us, in a funky, cheap hotel outside of Albuquerque, cable TV still new, we landed on the movie *The Accused* as we were flipping through channels. The evening had been sweet and silly. We ate at a dive restaurant for dinner and each had giant slices of pie for dessert, returning in high spirits to the hotel, where Wyatt and I had one room and Beck had an adjoining one.

We bid Beck good night and settled into the movie, which I'd never seen before, sitting propped up against the headboard of our hotel double bed. Wyatt had his arm around me when the film began, but by the time the full rape scene played out near the end, through the retelling of a bystander—Jodie Foster's character, Sarah, in a seedy, dimly lit bar, tipsy on beer, hair loose, tank top tight, denim skirt to her thighs, playing pinball with a couple of guys she'd just met—my entire posture had changed, and I'd pushed Wyatt's arm off me entirely without even knowing I'd done it.

"Oh, I love this song," Sarah says in the scene, and then starts dancing by herself, swiveling her hips, tank straps hanging off her shoulders, snapping her fingers. I started to feel physically ill. Then she's giggling, in this guy's arms, thinking she's still in control, still a human being, drunk or not, when he pushes her up against the pinball machine and lifts her skirt. I thought I might black out. Maybe I did. He starts to smother her, covering her mouth, shoving himself on her and in her, while the other men stand by and watch.

"Wait a minute, no," Sarah says when she realizes what is happening. His hands on her neck, he slams her head to the side, the pinball machine lights flashing behind her horror-stricken eyes, and then he rapes her. The camera switches to Sarah's POV, and we see her looking at the other men as they cheer her rapist on. We see a lone, nerdy, young-looking guy at the back of the room, his face turning from a game smile to terror as his moral compass resets in real time.

"Hold her down!" one man yells. Now another man is raping her, and then another. By then, I felt like I was floating outside my body. Finally, as the credits began to roll, Wyatt asked, "Are you OK?" No, I wasn't.

"That's what happened to my sister," I said, still unable to let him touch me.

I didn't anticipate having such a visceral reaction to the film, and it was really inconvenient because I was supposed to be having a lot of sex with my first love, who had flown over halfway across the country to be with me. But I couldn't even let Wyatt touch me, much less have sex.

The next morning I felt somewhat better and snuggled in toward Wyatt under the covers. "You know I would never hurt you," he said. "And I'm so sorry for what happened to your sister."

When he left after that visit in New Mexico, Beck and I forged on to San Francisco, but I knew that I didn't want to be away from him for another minute.

Beck, always game for whatever, among the many things I love about her, was not surprised by my change of heart, happy to see me so happy, and we hatched a plan together to drive back east without stopping or telling Wyatt, so that I could surprise him. Fifty-five hours later, I dropped Beck at her mom's in Massachusetts and drove another hour to Rye, New Hampshire, where Wyatt was renting a house on the beach with a roommate.

It was well past dark when I pulled into the driveway, and I could make out Wyatt's silhouette in the front door looking out to see who would be showing up to his house at this hour. He was on the phone, holding the receiver to his ear, wrenching his neck out toward the driveway. The ocean sent itself back and forth behind us, into the shore and into the night. I could hear the waves as I opened the door to get out of the car, and the pungent smell of seaweed flooded the air.

I started toward the house, which was on a slant, and climbed up the driveway, smiling through the splits of my cheeks, giddy that I'd managed to pull this off. When I was close enough that the porch light lit up my face, Wyatt dropped the receiver from his hand, stunned and then immediately elated, like the sky had opened up and started raining fantasies. It was then, and remains to this day, one of the best feelings I've ever felt.

I stayed over that night and never left. Wyatt's house in Rye was about thirty minutes from UNH, where he was finishing his junior year. Moving in with him was easy enough, since I owned little to nothing and Wyatt's roommate was very chill about everything so long as he could hear the waves, dude. Finding an apartment together in New Jersey for the summer proved more difficult. I let Wyatt take charge of the search—he knew the areas to look, while I was working a temporary waitressing job near Wyatt's apartment to save some money toward the move. I was working an afternoon lunch shift when the manager told me I had a call.

"Hey," Wyatt said, the sound of defeat resonant in his voice.

"What's wrong?" We'd only been together for only a few months, most of which had been spent on the phone, so I'd learned to read his voice even if he'd just uttered one word.

"So, the landlord on that apartment I thought would be good for us? That I wanted you to see?"

"Yeah," I answered, leaning against the wall in the kitchen

where the phone was hanging, bracing myself to hear that we'd lost the apartment to someone else because we were too young or didn't have enough credit or something like that.

"Well, the landlord, he doesn't want to rent to us, because, um, because you're black."

"What? How did he even know?"

"He asked, like, almost kiddingly, he was like, 'Your girlfriend's not black, is she? Ha ha.' Like, jokingly."

"Well, that's bullshit." I honestly didn't know what else to say. It was like that moment in high school when word spread that Nate's dad wouldn't allow him to take me to the prom because I'm black. Racism was something I was still learning how to feel, much less talk about.

"No, I know, I totally know. It is. Total bullshit."

Wyatt and I ended up in an apartment negotiated by Wyatt's dad, who was well connected in real estate and owned a reputable BMW car dealership, that Wyatt agreed to paint over the summer to help pay off the loan for the security deposit we needed to borrow. I took on two jobs, one in retail, one as a waitress. Our apartment was just outside of Princeton, New Jersey, in a town called Hightstown, and both my retail and waitressing jobs were centrally located on the main drag near the Princeton University campus.

We didn't really have any furniture between us, and couldn't afford to buy any. We had a double futon on the floor in our bedroom, where Wyatt insisted I have a writing desk. In the kitchen was a small round table, where I'd serve us chef salad and tuna casserole for dinner, all I knew how to prepare, after Wyatt finished a long day of painting and I clocked off at the clothing store or my lunchtime restaurant shift. In the living room we had another futon, plain-covered with a frame, as our couch, and a TV with a VCR, which felt a little fancy. We were playing house and we knew it.

Wyatt loved politics and satire, windsurfing, his mother, and the music of Steely Dan and Pat Metheny. We both liked to read and consider the fate of the world, but we were not a perfect match by any stretch. Mostly we talked about our families, and the strange coincidence with Sophie. He often talked about how he envied the ease with which Paul, his younger brother, an avid windsurfer like Wyatt, breezed through life. Paul, who was somehow perpetually tan while living year-round in New Jersey, with sun-bleached blond hair and blue eyes, shirked responsibility and hopped from job to job because he could—and practically lived on the beach.

Examples of "healthy" relationships were scant for me growing up. Dad's relationships with women were focused around his needs and desires, often making the needs and desires of the women he was involved with, including Mom, seem less important. I knew he loved Mom, but I also could not understand why he would risk, if not losing her outright, then hurting her so deeply, which I witnessed him do through his relationships with other women. Subsequently, I didn't actually know how I felt about the roles and rules of a relationship, and was generally flying by the seat of my pants.

Twenty-Nine

W*yatt's love felt like a stamp* of approval, and provided the same powerful passport I'd felt as a child with my parents. An attractive, wealthy white boy had chosen me, and was willing to walk hand in hand with me in public, take me to parties and restaurants and even his family's country club. I was once again the special black person I'd been in my parents' image growing up, and in company with the Tilsons. Not the ugly black girl whom Mrs. Gordon had referred to in the fifth grade, not the nigger like my boss in high school had called me, not the black girl Nate's father said he wouldn't want to be seen with in a picture.

My relationship with Wyatt was significant in a lot of ways, like most first loves, but perhaps more important, it gave me my first real glimpse at independence from Tess, who had initially been happy about Wyatt, but was also quick to remind me that first loves rarely last. "Your happiness," she said to me just before Wyatt and I moved in together, "only makes it more poignant for me that it will eventually end between the two of you."

The more I told Wyatt about my relationship with Tess—the backstory, the adoption and reunion—the more he thought the whole situation was unhealthy. I told him he didn't understand, protecting Tess instinctively, but also knowing somehow that he was right. "You need to figure this relationship out, Beck," Wyatt said one night when we were lying together on our modest little futon couch after dinner, one standing lamp nearby, mugs of tea in front of us on the rickety coffee table that we'd found at a flea market. "Because this is going to affect both of us, and our future together."

Hearing Wyatt talk about a future together made me feel emboldened, and forced me to examine my relationship with Tess more closely—especially after the first letter I received from her when Wyatt and I moved in together, which came with a xeroxed copy of a print interview with Toni Morrison and started like this:

> *I am sending the uppity, very uppity Toni Morrison interview. She comes across as arrogant, thoughtful, and seriously pissed off . . . I like her uppity answer to teenage pregnancies. I think I almost agree with it.*

I had fallen in love with Toni Morrison after reading *Sula* in Elijah's class at UNH, after which I went on to read everything of hers that I could get my hands on. Tess was well aware of this, and it seemed thoughtful at first that she was sending me the interview, despite the blatant racism of describing Morrison as "uppity." Tess's letter continued:

> *Saw Elijah the other day at the A&P. His wife was driving the car and he was a passenger. She parked and I parked near his car (I know this is childish, but I couldn't resist seeing him squirm) . . . and squirm he did. I got out of the car, he stayed in his, and I pranced my broadened hips past him, being tan in minimal summertime dress, knowing I was looking and seeming just fine. So I go into the store and come out, and look over to his car, and there he is . . . just about on all fours on the floor of his car. Well, not exactly. But what he had done was put the seat in a reclining position—his neck and head unnaturally poised flat*

against the horizontal seat, so he wouldn't see me and I wouldn't see him. Ha. I saw him, and I looked at him, and I kept seeing him, and he looked very close to paralyzed, because what if he moved or something? This, I can tell you, was fun.

Neither of us had mentioned Elijah again—the incident in the dean's office or that he even existed—until now.

Wyatt was absolutely floored when I showed it to him. "What the hell is wrong with her?"

That letter, Wyatt's concern, and the physical distance from her made me start to question everything about my nearly decade-long relationship with Tess in an even more rigorous and intentional way than I had been. Because what the hell *was* wrong with her? And perhaps even more pointedly, what was wrong with me for staying in this relationship with her, and still allowing her to hold such a powerful sway over me?

✦ *Thirty* ✦

Wyatt *drove me to Hadley, Massachusetts,* known as the Pioneer Valley, to start my first semester at Hampshire College as a transfer student in the fall of 1989. I was assigned to Dakin, one of the two flat, square dorms on campus, although most second- and third-year students lived in "mods," two-story apartments spread across campus in various clusters, each with its own title and identity. It didn't matter to me; I was primarily focused on getting what I had to get done to graduate, and taking care of my relationship with Wyatt, who drove the four hours from UNH almost every weekend to be with me during my first semester.

Hampshire was a tenth the size of UNH, and statistically not that much more diverse in terms of black students, but the size made black students more visible to one another, and although Dakin was mostly white, my classes, which included African history and Adoption and Society, were not. Two of my classes were taught by black professors, one of whom, Fred Brown, who was head of the School of Humanities, Arts and Cultural studies, became my advisor.

I kept my relationship with Fred very straightforward, not necessarily formal but definitely pragmatic. I didn't want to create a situation even slightly reminiscent of my relationship with Elijah, and was constantly mindful of keeping a healthy distance between us. I still didn't know whether my relationship with Elijah had been healthy, but I wasn't taking any risks this time. Fred had an Amiri Baraka afro, a bit of a bend in his posture, and a very soothing nature about him. He was a great listener who managed to take something you said, process it, and give it back to you as a gift, a means of encouragement.

My plan was to graduate in three years, even though many of my classes and traditional grades from UNH did not transfer for credit at Hampshire, which uses an evaluation-based curriculum divided into Divisions I, II, and III. I had enough credits to skip the Humanities & Arts Division I requirement, but still had to fulfill three others in the sciences. I found it all super exciting. Wyatt found it less so, and by the end of my first semester, our relationship was suffering.

"It's just that you seem so absorbed in your studies all of a sudden," Wyatt said over dinner at a restaurant near the UNH campus. I'd just completed the first semester at Hampshire, and was off for Christmas break. Tess invited me to stop in Newburyport, Massachusetts, where she and William had just bought a new house, on my way to stay with Wyatt in Durham for a night before heading up to Warner together to visit with my parents.

"To see your brothers," Tess said. "Mateo could really use a visit from his sister."

Ten-year-old Mateo had been acting out, badly and often, ever since he'd returned from a year living with Miguel on the Lower East Side of New York, which had not gone well. Ever since the first time I held him during that first visit to Tess's, when I was about the same age he was now, the two of us had always shared an intense bond, unspoken and hardwired. I never searched for a reason, only ever made myself available to him, and Sebastian, too, but to a lesser degree.

Sebastian had bonded with William while Mateo was away living in New York, and was, by all accounts, a happy, confident, sports-focused kid. Mateo, brown-skinned and cerebral, was often perceived as exotic, as I had been as a child—he was plagued by the same misconception that I was—and he didn't quite know how to come back to this family that had formed while he was away, who to be or how to develop his identity, racially or otherwise.

Tess frequently took advantage of our sibling bond when she was feeling overwhelmed or frustrated about how best to parent Mateo. When Mateo was in New York City, miserable and pleading with her to let him come home, she called me at UNH in a panic. "I think you have to go get him. You're the only one who can save him," she said. I remember getting the call one night, on the hall phone at Smith, and then driving into Portsmouth, where I sat with her in the kitchen, and we drank tequila and smoked cigarettes until she felt better about the situation.

Now, with Mateo entering into a tumultuous adolescence, I'd been called yet again to visit, for both of my brothers this time. Sebastian and I agreed that Mateo was in a really rough place, and expressed our concern to Tess. She listened, and then moved on. In a few days, I received a letter:

> *I know you and Sebastian worry about him. The lateral devotion and instinctive protectiveness of siblingness always floors me. (In my own situation as well.) But I must tell you that it's hardball time with M. Tough love city. A child simply cannot be allowed to tyrannize his living space as acutely as M has.*

My holiday visit with Tess and my brothers started out the same as all the others. I spent some alone time with each brother, talking with him about whatever was on his mind—sometimes we just goofed around. We joined Tess and William for dinner, during which we joked and laughed with one another, and as we were cleaning up after, Tess asked about how things were going with Wyatt.

"Fine, though he thinks I'm too focused on my classes," I said, handing her a dish to dry. "He thinks that I'm going to forget about him."

"Well, here's the thing with Bancroft women . . ." Tess said, gearing up for what I knew would be another quickly spun theory that planted her power and relevance squarely at the center of things. But whenever she used the term "Bancroft women," I felt like I couldn't unhear it, and I felt an automatic, involuntary pull to be in league with the "Bancroft women"—never described as anything else other than charismatic, gutsy, and appealing—and the Bancrofts in general, a lineage that Roy often referenced as well, intellectuals and anglophiles who "summered."

"The men in my life, our lives, are consumed by love for us, and they know we have lives that are important to us," Tess continued. "Our lovers know that they are, in essence, expendable."

The restaurant where Wyatt and I were having dinner the next night was cozy and dark, with strings of tiny white Christmas lights hung along the walls where they met the ceiling. I felt restless and anxious after visiting with Tess, as if I wasn't doing my relationship with Wyatt right.

"If I'm absorbed in my studies," I said, nursing a Diet Coke, "it's because they are important to me, and you, as my boyfriend, my partner, should understand that you are only as important as my studies. Because, ultimately, you are expendable." I found myself parroting Tess's words, almost verbatim.

Even though I didn't actually believe them. I didn't believe that the men we love were expendable. Yes, there should be equality in a relationship between two people, but there was something about Tess's phrasing that made it seem like men don't matter at all, which didn't resonate with me.

Certainly I'd seen that play out with the men in Tess's life. Her split with Miguel had been her decision, and when she was done, she was done, while Miguel appealed several times to try and make it work. This was how I remember her talking to me about my birth father, Joe—when she had decided things were over between them, she "closed that chapter" and moved on. In her relationship with William, it was clear that he adored her, and she loved him, though there was no mistaking that she had the upper hand. But I wasn't Tess.

Now that I said the words, though, I couldn't take them back.

Wyatt was visibly hurt, but didn't respond. What could he have possibly said?

Thirty-One

We had a large dry-erase board on the wall in the mod's common space where we wrote notes, and posted stickers and Post-its. I came in from class one afternoon to see a note pinned to the board written in my roommate's funky scrawl that read, in all caps: RYAN CALLED, WANTS YOU TO CALL HIM BACK.

I hadn't seen Ryan, my crush from middle and high school, since we'd run into each other over Christmas break during our first year in college, so it was a surprise to hear from him now. I knew, though, that he was at Wesleyan, about an hour from Hampshire, and I called him back, missing him, curious to know how his life was going. He invited me to come visit and see this "really impressive" black choir perform. I found it both weird and flattering that he called, and even more so that he wanted to see me. I was curious, too, so I accepted his invitation and drove to Middletown, Connecticut, one Friday after classes to meet him at Wesleyan for the concert.

Ryan looked the same, boyish and beautiful, although he also appeared more engaged. We'd never had conversations about race or my being black in high school. Ryan had been into soccer, Bliss, and his schoolwork, which is not to say that he wasn't smart, but more that he distanced himself from me when these conversations started to matter. He knew about Nate's father and the prom incident, but never said anything to me about it.

The concert was lovely, the choir divine and urgent, their harmony an arresting cultural cadence, although the audience was mostly white, an observation I expressed over coffee at a community center on campus afterward.

"I don't think it's fair to suggest that all the white people in the audience were racist," Ryan said, his words fat and presumptuous, taking up all the space clear across the table between us.

I was aghast since that wasn't even close to what I'd said. "I didn't suggest that at all," I interjected. "I said it's unnerving to be at a concert by a black choir, and for me, as a black person, to see that the audience is almost entirely white people."

"But what do you mean by 'unnerving'? The white people in the audience were there to hear the music, why is that a problem?" Ryan said, both our coffees untouched, his self-assuredness alarming. "How is that unnerving?"

"You really just don't think about this stuff at all, do you?

"What stuff?"

"Like, race and identity and racism. You don't see how privileged you are, and all these rich, preppy white kids around you who don't have to think about racism, or being the only one in a room, or the target of racism every day."

"Well, what about reverse racism? You talk about these so-called rich, preppy white kids with such contempt and righteousness. Like, all of a sudden white people are expected to know how to assimilate into a race-conscious environment. I feel like there should be some sort of support group for us to figure it out, and not be judged while we do it."

"A white support group for white people to vent their ignorance about race? Are you serious?" My ire was rising rapidly. "Oh, boo-hoo. Listen, Ryan, you are twenty-one years old, and if you can't find a way to educate yourself, do a little research, and get over it without a white support group, you're screwed. We're all screwed."

"I don't think I should be punished for never having been exposed to racism growing up," he said, with a touch of exasperation.

"Jesus, Ryan. You could have asked me."

He looked at me with an air of pure, unadulterated arrogance. "It never occurred to me."

I slept on the floor of Ryan's room that night, restless and cold with just a blanket and pillow, too angry to ask for more, and woke early the next day to drive back to Hampshire without saying goodbye. I was mad at myself for going, for giving any credence to his opinion, and for allowing myself to be flattered by his invitation. But I was even madder at him. *What an idiot*, I thought. I realized that my visit with Ryan had inspired in me a surety about my blackness that, as Elijah had once said of my writing, was "gaining steam."

✤ Thirty-Two ✤

Ironically, I had been the one to encourage Wyatt to start writing in a journal. I'd given him one for Christmas, and was glad to see him writing, something he'd expressed a vague interest in pursuing as a career. In March, I drove to Durham, where Wyatt was now sharing another rental, this time closer to campus, to talk face-to-face.

Things had been strained since our Christmas-break dinner, when I'd told him he was expendable. I'd since apologized about what I said, and thought we'd moved on, but he was still distant and irritable when we talked on the phone. I asked him numerous times what was going on with him, with us, but he just said he had a lot on his mind. So I decided to make a concerted effort to show him how much he meant to me, and surprise him with a visit just as I'd done the year before when I changed my cross-country plans.

It was late when I arrived, and he seemed happy to see me. We had sex, which, for us, was the great connector. While he was in the shower the next morning, I rolled over to his side of the bed, a queen mattress and box spring, and hung my head over the side; the sheet smelled musty, and I knew Wyatt probably hadn't changed it in weeks. And there it was, his journal, the one I'd given him, a simple gray hardcover with red binding. I reasoned that if he wasn't going to tell me what was going on, I was going to find out on my own.

I squinted my eyes to read his blocky, half-cursive, half-print handwriting, feeling a love toward the familiarity of it from notes and cards and love letters he'd sent over the past year. I randomly flipped to a page in the middle of the book, and my stomach dropped.

My love for her is dishonest, the entry started. It went on to say that he only loved me because I was beautiful, and was trying to figure out why he had been so drawn to me in the first place. I was sitting on the edge of the bed, my back to the bathroom, where I didn't even hear the shower turn off, reading in disbelief, when Wyatt came into the room with a towel wrapped around his waist.

"What are you doing?" Wyatt said angrily.

"What is this?" I said, tears streaming down my face.

"Oh God, Beck, listen," he said, more tenderly now, as he sat down next to me on the side of the bed and tried to hug me, but I flinched.

"When were you going to tell me? Was any of it real?"

The whole scene was so cliché, like a bad made-for-TV movie. But also absolutely devastating.

"Yes, I mean, sort of," Wyatt said. "I'm just trying to figure out what I want, you know? You always seem so clear about what you want, and I just, I don't know. I think we should take some time apart."

"Are you breaking up with me?" I said, through melted, murmured words and tears.

"I guess so?" This was Wyatt, though. Nothing was over until it was over. A pragmatist through and through.

I cried the whole way back to Hampshire, listening to Steely Dan's *Gaucho* album over and over in my car's cassette player. When I arrived back to my dorm, puffy-eyed and distraught from grieving the breakup of my first love and first relationship, I realized that I had no real community there, no close friends or girlfriends to help me through it. My girlfriends from youth—Leah, Monique, and Beck—were all occupied with their own lives. I could have called, but a phone conversation seemed like effort, and a disruption I didn't want to cause.

Leah was pregnant with her first child and had left Oberlin to move back to New Hampshire, where she planned to raise her child in close proximity to his father, a black man who lived in Vermont, and his extended family there. Monique was living in Boston with her boyfriend from college and getting ready to apply to law school, while Beck was studying biomedical science at Cornell.

I had a single room in Dakin, and spent the next two days holed up there by myself, wallowing in my misery. One friend left a cup of granola and yogurt in front of my door, which I left untouched. When I reemerged to finish up classes, I felt like my heart had been stripped of its arteries. Tess's words rang in my head, as usual: *Your happiness only makes it more poignant for me that it will eventually end between the two of you.* That she was right only intensified my heartbreak.

I spent the whole summer trying to get over Wyatt. We slept together a number of times, after which I always left in tears. It was a way for me to feel wanted, and for Wyatt to indulge whatever fantasy version of me he was still trying to figure out—occasionally I felt like he was trying to work out the shame he felt around treating his black adopted sister badly. Other times, it seemed he just couldn't comprehend how or why he found me attractive.

✢ Thirty-Three ✢

I returned to Hampshire that fall, this time to live in a mod instead of the dorm, ready to put Wyatt behind me. Mod life turned out to be just what I needed.

In Mod 42, our three-bedroom apartment in the Enfield housing area, I lived with three other women, each spirited and smart in her own way, all white, from working-class, academic, or artistic families. They were curious and inclusive, gay and bi and queer, good-humored and kind. We cooked together every night, and read to one another sometimes, talked about ways to make the world better, and how they could be allies to me as white feminists.

Back at Dakin, my room had been so small there wasn't enough wall space to hang art or posters. In Mod 42, my room on the first floor was a good size, large even, with a big, built-in desk and plenty of wall space, where I hung my favorite poster, the iconic "Playground" image of Michael Jordan playing on the blacktop against a wall of colorful graffiti, mid-jump on his way to the basket for a dunk, surrounded by Nike-clad kids in motion, their shoulders barely reaching Jordan's ankles.

It's an arresting, joyful, and poetic image that was a way to keep my blackness, and black greatness, in full sight. I bought a small throw rug with vibrant oranges, yellows, and reds to cover the nasty gray carpeting, and a bright red butterfly chair that I put between my desk and the bed. It was cozy and it felt like mine, a space that I alone had made.

I completed my Division I work, and homed in on what I needed to do for my Division II, which usually consisted of a year or two of designated coursework and research in preparation for Division III, essentially a written dissertation to be presented to a committee and defended in your final year. In an advanced black literature class with Fred, I discovered Audre Lorde, who had gone unintroduced in my class with Elijah at UNH, and read her seminal essay, "Uses of the Erotic: Erotic as Power," which became the impetus for my Division III, a collection of interviews with black women writers.

I reconnected with a guy from Botswana named Kigosi I'd met in my African history class during my first semester but had not pursued a friendship with, despite his clear interest in one. I'd been too focused on Wyatt. Kigosi led me to the Prescott mod area, which I finally learned, in my third semester at Hampshire, was broadly known as the mod area where all the black folks lived.

I had been curious about where the black students in my classes lived on campus, but I never asked because, it finally occurred to me one warm afternoon in the quad, sitting with Kigosi and a few other black students on the steps to the library, when a group of white students walked by, that being with black people meant not being with white people, and vice versa. I wasn't equipped to be in a white relationship, or in any white-centric dynamic, and also invite blackness other than my own. I didn't have the tools to fluidly navigate both worlds.

Wyatt recognized my blackness in a superficial way. We went to see Miles Davis in concert, and *Do the Right Thing* at the movies. He gave me an Alice Walker book on our first Valentine's Day together, and made me a tape of Joan Armatrading when I started at Hampshire, but we never talked about any of these concerts or movies or books or the issues they raised, and had no black friends. Apart from Sophie, who was struggling with her own identity, we didn't socialize with black people. We didn't even spend that much time with Sophie.

I had no model for how to integrate these two "warring ideals," as W. E. B. Du Bois referred to it in his classic book, *The Souls of Black Folk*, until I met Elijah, who introduced me both to Du Bois and his concept of "double consciousness," which only resonated now that I found myself trying to figure out why I'd never known where all the black folks lived at Hampshire. But then Elijah's model had been corrupted by Tess. So I continued to adapt, or assimilate, still without the language to express or truly understand what I was experiencing.

Ryan called again and invited me to come back to visit him at Wesleyan. This time, he said, we could talk about my experience in high school—he wanted to understand, and was sorry if he'd come across as ignorant or dismissive during our last visit. We went out to dinner at a nice restaurant off campus, and even before we'd polished off a bottle of wine, Ryan was attentive, intentionally flirtatious with me for the first time in the ten years we'd known each other. And I knew exactly why.

I was wearing a pair of faded, oversized 501 Levi's jeans, cinched tight at the waist to emphasize how tiny I'd become, and a boxy jade green cropped cotton sweatshirt from the clothing store where I worked. My hair was a cascade of loose curls, snatched back with a band just past my forehead and tucked behind my ears.

I'd been controlling my eating off and on since high school— sometimes I would starve myself; other times I would binge. A sort of cross between anorexia and bulimia. The latter always failed because I only ever binged, never purged. Tess, whose body shape was more pearlike than mine, which turned curveless and rectangular when I got very skinny, insisted that our bodies be in a constant symbiotic dance. This meant that if she thought her thighs were too big, then my thighs were too big. If she wanted to go on a diet, I went on a diet.

I was keenly aware that the ultimate goal was always to be thin, skinny. That's what beauty meant. That's what whiteness rewarded. Everywhere I looked. In the months leading up to this visit with Ryan, I'd been in one of my starving phases.

"Why weren't you this into me when we were in high school?" I asked on our way back to his dorm, when he'd come up from behind me, grabbed my waist, and kissed my neck. He playfully leaned me up against a concrete wall in the quad, and lifted me up to sit, positioning himself in between my thighs. "Is it because I'm, like, fifteen pounds lighter than I was when we were in high school?"

Ryan nuzzled his face further into my neck. "Maybe," he said unrepentantly.

I was in no way surprised. I'd starved myself to be skinny for the specific purpose of appealing to Ryan, and other white boys.

That night, while Ryan was on top of me, I wondered if he was pretending I wasn't black, or, worse, pretending I was.

Thirty-Four

I'd walked by the Greenhouse mod a thousand times. It was the mod with the highest profile on campus; everyone knew about the Greenhouse and the residents it attracted—mostly rich, white liberal kids from wealthy towns and private schools on the coasts of the country. It felt enormously familiar to me, and appealing in a Pavlovian way.

Molly, a pretty blonde with glacial-blue eyes whom I'd seen before but never met, was sitting on the front steps of the Greenhouse, in tears.

"Are you OK?" I asked, genuinely concerned.

"Yeah," she said, laughing through her tears. "It's dumb."

"I'm sure it's not," I said, and sat down next to her.

"Well, it's about a guy, so . . ."

"What's his deal?"

"It's not worth it," Molly said, her red fleece Patagonia zipped up to her chin.

But without much further persuasion, it all came out, all the details about her recent breakup with a guy who sounded an awful lot like Wyatt.

"Oof," I said, as if falling back into my native language. "I've been there. Totally."

Molly and I bonded over our broken, rich, WASPy ex-boyfriends. Even though Molly herself came from rich, WASP heritage, having this experience in common with her reminded me of how I felt when Ella invited me to sit at the popular table in the sixth grade. It was power-adjacent, which made me feel validated, while simultaneously feeling as if adjacency was all I could ever aspire toward.

Molly and I also each had a problematic parent whom we were forever trying to understand, whose expectations we never seemed to meet, but whose love and acceptance we wanted more than anything. For Molly, it was her dad, a brusque businessman who worked in the pharmaceutical industry and frowned on his daughter's lack of direction or plans for the future.

Mid-semester, Molly invited me to her house in Connecticut to get away from school for the weekend, and I couldn't deny that a weekend in the country appealed to me. Her house was a lavish single-family colonial with a pool in the back and a long turn-around driveway, set in a residential area about a mile and a half from Martha Stewart's two-acre estate. Even in late fall, the neighborhood had the feel of a summer resort, with sprawling lawns out front, every house white, surrounded by neatly lined stone walls or well-manicured hedges.

Everything in the house was both neatly organized and overabundant, with piles of freshly laundered clothes and unopened packages stacked up on the stairs, rows of the same kind of chips and snacks on the shelves, and an elaborate antique dollhouse that took up an entire room. Molly's mother, fetching with soft brown hair and lambent eyes, wore resignation like a weighty antique necklace, beautiful but tarnished, while Molly's father was, as she had described, hardened and not particularly warm or welcoming.

"So what are you studying?" he asked, not long into my visit.

"Black literature," I said. "And writing." Molly was in the kitchen busying herself, which appeared to be the way it went when she visited home—finding things to do to make herself useful, as an alternative to talking.

"What do you plan to do with that?"

I almost asked him if he was taunting me, but decided to be a polite guest for as long as I could. "Well, I'm hoping to change the way people think about race and racism, and especially black women, through writing."

Molly's father chuckled dismissively.

"It's not really funny," I said.

"You just sound so serious, so angry," he said.

"Well, that's because I *am* angry."

"But you're getting the same education as Molly is getting, so what's there to be angry about?"

"Dad," Molly interrupted.

"What? It's true," he said. His words hurled toward Molly, whose body took the blow and seemed to sink back a bit.

This was now the second time within a year I'd found myself answering to or being judged by the wealthy white parent of someone with whom I'd chosen to be in a relationship. Although Wyatt's mother mostly filtered her harsh criticism and coded racism through Wyatt—telling him I gave off a "sexually promiscuous" vibe, and that I was too controlling and self-righteous—Molly's father was openly baiting me.

"That's a trope, you know," I said. "The angry black woman."

"But you just said yourself that you're angry, and I want to know why."

"Can we not do this," Molly said.

"I was just curious," her father said.

Later Molly apologized on her father's behalf, and said he didn't mean to be rude. I didn't know how to tell her that he hadn't merely been rude; he'd been racist, presumptuous, and patronizing. Even if I had, I'm almost sure she would not have been able to hear it. And for a while, I thought that was OK.

✦ Thirty-Five ✦

Dear Rebecca, you seem unfamiliar lately, almost passive, which I would
have never thought you to be . . . This new attitude makes me think
you are trying on different ways to be, and that this way resembles more
your parents' demeanor.

So began a letter I received from Tess after months of no cor-
respondence between us.

Tess's presumption that I wasn't able to do anything independent of her without defaulting to the child my parents raised
was self-serving and mean-spirited, and I didn't know what to
say anymore. This was happening more and more, and was why
I increasingly kept my distance. I wrote back and kept it simple,
saying I hoped things were well with her, and that I was busy with
school and work, ready to get through the semester. She wrote
back right away.

There is something oddly familiar about our being apart . . .
comfortable even. Perhaps being separated, yearning, quietly, from time
to time for each other is our natural state . . . Life is good in NBPT.
Uncomfortably perfect, in fact. The house is an amazing gift; large,
colorful, comfortable, begging to hold lots of people (which it has and

continues to) . . . The economy is a mess, but people are buying books
and we are without much worry.

> *The kids are blooming, blossoming, adjusting so well. Sebastian*
had Little League tryouts for next year and was first pick of 45 boys.
He's my most favorite athlete to watch. One of the coaches said he was
"smooth" and that's exactly what he is. He's taking saxophone lessons
and looks tremendously sexy with the alto sax slung around his neck,
perched on his hip. He gets his braces off in five weeks, and I think then
he will be too beautiful.

> *Mateo is at his best. He's found his stride, it appears. He is a*
super student—all A's and B's. . . . Also, he is, apparently, dreamboat
extraordinaire among 7th and 8th grade girls . . . We were grocery
shopping the other day, and this blonde number (like long curls and
tight britches), oh about 5ft-two, kept yelling his name and waving,
and I thought, Oh, one of his teachers. Well, no, boys and girls, it was
an eighth grader who has been asking him out since the beginning of
school . . . Another girl followed him home yesterday.

The way she described the boys was absolutely nuts to me, not least of all because of how explicitly and harshly she had judged my parents for telling me I was beautiful as a child. But the way she sexualized my brothers, at eleven and twelve years old, was deeply unsettling.

I put it all out of my mind and was happy to have both mental and physical distance from Tess. Three thousand miles to be exact. Moving to San Francisco was a fresh start I needed. I was thrilled to start a spring internship at *Mother Jones*, and excited to dig deeper into the idea of becoming a writer.

It was an amazing opportunity to work for the progressive magazine, but it paid only a very small stipend, and I was constantly trying to make ends meet. I lived in three different apartments over the course of four months, starting with an apartment on Lombard Street with Wyatt, who drove across the country to try to make things work with us again. He seemed conflicted, desperate to come, but it wasn't the same. It would never be the same.

Wyatt and I lived together in a newly rebuilt, post–1989 San Francisco earthquake apartment with shiny hardwood floors and tall windows for two tumultuous months before he decided to drive back East. He hadn't been able to find work, and was running out of savings; we fought all the time and didn't know what we were doing. Wyatt decided that he would go back home, work for his father to make some more money, and then we could decide what we wanted to do next.

But a month later, Wyatt called from his mother's house in New Jersey and broke up with me for good over the phone. He was tired of me, he said. And I could understand. I was tired of me, too. Tired of wanting and wishing I could be the kind of girlfriend that Wyatt didn't have to figure out why he was attracted to. Tired of feeling like a fraud in khaki pants worn low around my waist like the models in J.Crew catalogs, when I could get skinny enough. Tired of being the black woman deemed valuable only because I was in a relationship with a white guy.

"Just think about how awful it was when you were living together and fighting all the time," Mom said, on the other end of the phone when I told her about the breakup. She was right. Wyatt and I had spent the two months together in San Francisco fighting about money and work and time spent together and the future and our families. But in between his leaving and his calling to break up with me, we wrote each other long, detailed love letters. Wyatt didn't know why he loved me, and all I wanted was to be loved. He couldn't understand my racial anxiety, and I couldn't see past his powerfully white indemnity.

After Wyatt left, I moved to another apartment, in San Francisco's Mission District. My two roommates were the owner, a white woman juggler with the famed Pickle Family Circus, and a nice young white guy who was getting a master's at San Francisco State. I walked the mile or so to the *Mother Jones* offices in South of Market every day and passed a health food store in between, where I stopped frequently enough to meet and befriend Ellis, a black actor, producer, and writer working at the store to support his art.

Ellis invited me to see him in a stage performance of *Dutchman*, by Amiri Baraka, the Black Arts Movement poet and writer formerly known as LeRoi Jones. I'd never seen or read the play before, and it blew my mind. Baraka wrote it in 1964, when the idea of a black middle class was still nascent, Martin Luther King was more prevalent than Malcolm X, and three years before *Loving v. Virginia*, the landmark Supreme Court decision that made interracial marriage legal.

In *Dutchman*, a one-act play set in a New York City subway car, Clay, a middle-class black man, is seduced by fellow passenger Lula, a white woman who intentionally provokes Clay to anger and then kills him. It illustrated to me, in one fell, trenchant, and vicious swoop, the insidious nature of anti-black racism, and the protected, vaunted purity and power of white women in America. To me, Lula, the white female protagonist, represented not just America, in that her sole purpose in the story is to seduce, corrupt, and destroy Clay, the black male protagonist, but also Tess, in her endless attacks on my psyche as a black girl and now woman. The play articulated for me through Clay's character how I had been complicit in what I now understood to be Tess's seduction and psychological manipulation.

Ellis, average height, with deep, chestnut-brown skin, and a comely face, gave a pulsating, nuanced performance as Clay. Clay is drawn to Lula immediately, because proximity to her whiteness and femininity is, to his mind, the crowning achievement of his assimilation as a black man on America's terms. But his proximity also induces fear in Clay, given the brutal, bloody history of black men looking at white women, much less sitting and chatting with one.

I was captivated by the actress who played Lula, as she baited and dismissed and poured herself all over Ellis, both actors giving such strong performances that in one instance, I had to stop myself from running up onto the stage to shake Ellis out his trance, yank him out from under the white gaze. To save him. To save myself. Lula was Tess. Tess was Lula.

Ellis and I stayed up late that night talking in his apartment about the play, and how great it would be if we could collaborate on another adaptation, but this time for screen, and I would write the screenplay and direct, and Ellis would star. The warm light of yellowed lampshades, little and large jade trees lining his apartment windows, '70s beaded doorway into the kitchen, and worn, light brown leather couch made it all feel like a theater set, and we laughed and dreamed and drank our tea.

I told Ellis about my forthcoming piece for *Mother Jones*, my first for the magazine, an interview with Talking Heads front man David Byrne, about a world music label he was launching, Luaka Bop, and we talked about writing.

"It's everything," Ellis said. "*Every*thing."

"I know," I said, now thinking steadily about all the things I would write. "My head is exploding! Let's collaborate on everything!"

"Yes! You'll be an amazing writer, and we're going to be a marvelous team!"

In an entirely coincidental turn of events, a few months after Wyatt left San Francisco, Ryan flew out to visit me and other friends for a few days and to interview for a job working with special needs kids. We spent a day together at the Exploratorium, the city's public laboratory of science and art, listening to music made from spools of thread and paper clips, staring through telescopes and making strange recordings of our own voices. We didn't bring up sleeping together the fall before, or the conversation at Wesleyan about the black choir and reverse racism.

I didn't want to talk about anything serious. I didn't want to think about race. I just wanted to hold hands with my crush from the sixth grade and walk around an enormous space with high, arched ceilings, like the inside of a parachute, feeling the way I used to feel when I was little and Mom and Dad would carry the dining room table outside and we would eat our dinner under the night sky.

Thirty-Six

S*hortly after the internship ended, and* I returned back East, Ryan moved to Northern California for the job he'd applied for when I still lived there. He'd been in Berkeley for less than a month when I asked him to come back to the East Coast, because, I wrote, I might be in love with him. I couldn't stop thinking about that day we'd spent together at the Exploratorium in San Francisco, holding hands, playful and sweet, his full attention like a familiar balm, a gift, what I'd been waiting for since I was eleven years old.

I want to fight for us, I wrote. *Like I wanted to in high school after you started dating Bliss, but I was too angry and hurt. I have dreams where we see each other from afar and run into each other's arms as though it's been decades, as though our lives and the beat of our hearts depend on us finding and holding each other in that moment.*

The letters I wrote were romantic and seductive. I was *trying* to seduce him, and it worked.

Ryan flew in from Berkeley and arrived late at night in Cambridge, where I was housesitting for Roy and Claire while they summered in Durham, New Hampshire.

"I want you to be my environment," he said as we lay together in the dark.

His environment? I thought. What the hell did that even mean?

It made me feel like I was a project and not a person. As if he still didn't, or couldn't, actually see me.

The next day we visited my parents in Warner, and then went to a community play his mother, Ann, had helped put together at our old high school. I was wearing a bright orange tank dress and a pair of sandals that kept falling off only my right heel. We crossed the old parking lot, holding hands, Ryan waiting as I stopped to slip my shoe back on; it was the same parking lot where I'd leave fifth period in Ryan's borrowed car so that I could escape his giddy young love with Bliss.

Inside the high school, people were gathered in the cafeteria just outside of the auditorium, and Ann greeted us, grinning proudly. She grabbed Ryan's arm and pulled us over to meet a conservative-looking white couple. "This is my son, Ryan," she beamed, almost maniacally. "And this is his girlfriend, Rebecca," Ann said, as if I was a newly appraised object on view, once thought to be valueless but now possibly worth millions. I knew then that I wouldn't be able to go through with it.

Suddenly, I saw dinners and family gatherings and holidays that would play out just like this if Ryan and I stayed together. His mother would take pride in how she had ultimately come to accept her son's black girlfriend, and her important white friends would look at her, then at me and us, with polite discomfort, while an internal struggle played out over how best to pretend they accepted an interracial relationship when black people still weren't even allowed at many country clubs in America.

I was having an awakening that Ryan couldn't possibly understand: taking pride in my blackness did not depend on white approval or proximity. For years, maybe my whole life up until then, I had only ever thought of my blackness in the context of whiteness—my family, Mrs. Gordon, Tess, Nate, Mr. James, my boss at the oil company, Wyatt, and now Ryan. Even when I'd established connections to black people—Mrs. Rowland, the boys at the Speakeasy, Elijah—white people controlled those relationships and, in most cases when Tess was involved, sabotaged them.

Ryan stayed with his parents that night, and I stayed with mine. The next day we met at an outdoor café in New London, where I'd asked him to meet me.

"I thought I could do it, but I can't," I said.

"You're making a mistake," Ryan said.

"I'm sorry. I love you, I do, but it just feels wrong," I told him, wishing I could explain to him why I had to save myself from his whiteness, which suddenly felt so suffocating to me. But I already felt like I might change my mind again, and that would have been enormously unfair. The only thing I knew in that moment was that I had to hold on to myself, my blackness.

"It just *feels* wrong? You and your instincts and your beautiful fucking letters and your *righteousness*, my God. Maybe you should listen to my instincts this time. I think we'd make an amazing team."

I couldn't trust myself to invest in another white relationship without losing my sense of self, without tricking myself into believing that his stamp of approval gave me strength, as I'd thought with Wyatt, when it really just made me feel less black.

A few weeks later, I got a call from Tess. There had been postcards and brief notes between us, but we hadn't seen each other for nearly a year. We met at a restaurant in Harvard Square, and Tess said she'd been thinking maybe we should collaborate on a book together, which oddly, or perhaps not so oddly, kind of made sense to me at first. A co-memoir, of sorts, she said, about adoption and reunion.

The tone between us was cordial and cautious, like the first meeting after an agreed-upon trial separation between spouses that may or may not end up in divorce. "I'm actually not feeling that great about adoption or reunion at the moment," I told her over a salad I barely touched. For most of the summer I had subsisted on a small low-fat yogurt during my lunch break from the bookstore where I was working, something like steamed broccoli with a splash of tamari for dinner, and laxatives. I had a routine, and a salad, however few in calories, would mess that up.

"But think of all the people going through what we're going through," Tess said. "This book would be for them." She looked serene, well loved, and, as always at the height of summer, tan.

"I'll think about it," I said.

Walking through Harvard Square after lunch, back toward Roy and Claire's, where Tess had parked, I saw Michael, a familiar face from campus, coming toward us just past the Au Bon Pain to our right. I was wearing a faded green, short cotton T-shirt dress, with a long-sleeve chambray shirt tied low and tight around the forced slenderness of my hips. Up close, his eyes were nearly the same color as my dress.

"Hey," I said.

"Hey yourself," Michael said, his smile pushing wider, thick red-red lips set inside a toffee brown face.

"You home for the summer? You were off last semester, right?"

"Yeah," he said. "Staying with Moms. Tryna gather myself up for next semester."

"Oh, you coming back?"

"Yeah"—unabashedly looking at me like he wanted to devour me whole.

"Well, OK then," I said. "Cool."

"I'll look you up when I get to campus," he said, still grinning.

I nodded and turned to leave, having forgotten entirely that Tess was there.

"Who was *that*?" Tess asked.

"That's Michael Ladd," I said. "He's a poet and rap artist, his mom is the director of the Bunting Institute here in Cambridge."

"Well, I guess we know what you'll be doing this semester."

We laughed, like we used to, because we both knew she was right.

⊹ Thirty-Seven ⊹

Sure enough, a few weeks later when I got back to campus, I saw Michael in front of the library, and we spent the afternoon together talking about books and art, where we were from and what we thought about Hampshire. We laughed at how white and bourgie it was, and laughed even harder at how easily we ourselves had blended in.

We went from a couple afternoon talks in the quad to the tiny single mattress on the floor in my room almost before the season had time to change from summer to fall. I was smitten. One night early on in our relationship, Michael read the Langston Hughes poem "I Play It Cool" to me over the phone, and I thought he could lift my body with the sheer timbre of his voice, so potent and full.

Michael was plainly gorgeous, elegant-looking, with soft, resplendent skin and a crown of dark curls, loose and large. His voice was gravelly and ancient, like something between a Beat poet and an African griot. We were both studying black literature, and shared Fred as an academic advisor. There are no classes for final-year students at Hampshire, so I was writing and working on my Division III, while Michael, who still had another year to go, was taking courses in black poetry and history and music.

Not long into the semester, Michael performed live in front of a big crowd at a major music venue in Northampton, rapping his own verses with a band he'd put together, and I stood in the audience, awestruck, cheering and clapping and hooting wildly. *THIS is the one*, I thought. *He's IT.*

Like me, he had one black biological parent, Claudia, and one white biological parent, his father, who died when Michael was young. Technically, we both were biracial, but while I was still struggling with where to put or how to manage the biracial part of my identity, there was no questioning Michael's blackness. That's where I wanted to get, I thought, that resolute confidence and self-awareness that comes with being black, owning it, and will-fully denouncing white supremacy. In the same way that Elijah had taught me there was more than one way to be black, Michael taught me, and more important made me feel, that who I was was black enough.

Among other things, like rap music that could be both lyri-cal and cogent, Michael introduced me to fucking. Like real, un-abashed, sweaty, gorgeous *fucking*. And we did a lot of it. With Wyatt, the only other guy I'd had sex with on a regular basis over an extended period of time, sex felt like something that could keep us fastened together. It was always emotional and meaning-ful, but it didn't make my skin burn and ache the way it did when Michael and I had sex, like a language we made together, a carnal vernacular that took shape around the words he wrote and the way I received them.

Michael could be moody, though, and distant. And he drank heavily, which only made his mood swings more severe. A week could go by when I spoke with him only once or twice on the hall phone, or he'd show up to my room drunk late at night, banging on my door, his voice on the verge of breaking. At the time, I was not drinking, and had very little patience for his binges. Sometimes I'd let him in and hold his heavy, hard-headed crown in my lap until he fell asleep or passed out. Other times I shouted through the door for him to go away, and after a while, he would.

Thirty-Eight

*L*ottie was the first black girlfriend I'd had since Jazmine in Portsmouth, a friendship that hadn't lasted much past our talent show performance in DC, and the first black girlfriend to grease my scalp. Like Ida when I was twelve, Lottie looked at my hair, sighed, and shook her head. "Sit down, girl," she said, pointing to the floor in front of the couch in her mod's common space. I sat, and she left the room, coming back with a giant jar of shea butter and a comb.

Lottie sat behind me, with me in between her knees, and pulled my forehead back to start at my edges. She parted my hair in sections with the comb, tugging not too hard but not too soft either, and ran her index finger down through the line of bare scalp with a generous dab of shea butter. It felt so immediately ritualistic, like a necessary chore and an act of love, that I didn't mind the tugging.

We sat quietly together for an hour or more, Lottie working her fingers through my hair and scalp, while I let my head move in the direction she was pulling it. "There," she said when she was done. "We need to do this again in a couple of weeks, OK?"

I'd met Lottie through Michael, along with Deja and Ruby, three black girls who were active in Umoja, Hampshire's organization for students of color. I quickly became friends with this forthright, funny, and charismatic woman, who brought me up to speed on Umoja and myself. Lottie was studying textile art, and introduced me to black artists like Adrian Piper and Faith Ring-gold, and had absolutely no problem whatsoever letting me know that when I first started at Hampshire, all the black folks referred to me as "the black girl who thinks she's white."

My lip started to quiver a little when Lottie first told me that, and she quickly added, "Hey, girl. You don't need to feel bad about that now. I'm just telling you the truth. We can't grow without the truth." I nodded and let her hug me.

I never thought I was white, I wrote in my journal the night Lottie told me what the other black students had said. *I am aware that I was raised in an all-white environment, but I always knew I was not white. . . . I know that I will not, and I repeat, will not, have white kids or mixed kids—no way. I won't do it to them.* I wonder now if I remembered then the essay I wrote when I was six that started with, *I am a black child.*

Molly didn't like Lottie, because she felt threatened by her personality, and Lottie most certainly did not like Molly, because Molly was everything she hated about so many college-aged white girls, especially at our expensive private school, which Lottie and I both attended on scholarship—wealthy, self-involved, didn't know any black people other than the ones she selected to know on her own terms, played Ultimate Frisbee, and drove a pretentious car.

"If I'm being honest, though, your friendship with her is about that white-girl shit you're always trying to detach yourself from. You still think white is right."

"I mean, she's . . ." I was suddenly at a loss for words to list a single one of Molly's redeeming qualities. "Funny. She's funny."

"I'm not blaming you. The forces of white supremacy are strong," Lottie said plainly. "I'm just saying that one of the reasons folks said that shit about you thinking you're white is because you hang out with *a lot* of white people."

"Less than I used to," I said, in my defense.

"OK, girl." Lottie shook her head and gave me a half smile.

Again, I found myself pulled between two worlds, although Lottie telling me about the way black students had perceived me when I first arrived on campus, telling me about myself, for that matter, and the sheer bliss I felt with Michael had tipped the scales toward what always felt like the visceral pull of blackness and black community.

It's why I became active with Umoja, the politics and efforts of diversifying the school, and saw less and less of Molly, who had started to spend time with a golden boy around campus named Canaan.

Canaan was rakish and handsome, the son of a famous artist in New York, and had been involved with Lottie long before he and Molly became friendly. At a party we were all at toward the end of the semester, Lottie and I got into a deep conversation with Canaan about art; then Lottie left, and it was just me and Canaan talking. Molly approached me the next day to say she thought I'd been "inconsiderate" in the way I monopolized all of Canaan's time at the party.

The subtext in her condescending tone and expression was clear to me: *Just because Canaan went out with one black girl doesn't mean he'd want to go out with you.* But how was I monopolizing someone simply by being in conversation with him? A conversation that had been going on with more than one person before it became just between us?

I was offended and angry, but didn't want to get into it with her, so I just walked away.

"That bitch really tried it," Lottie said when I told her what Molly had said to me. "I don't know why you're friends with her. That white girl will *never* have your back. Trust."

Back on campus after the Christmas break, which I had spent in Warner with Mom and Dad as usual, Molly slipped a note under my door. I had consciously been avoiding her for some time. The note read: *What's going on? We haven't spoken in weeks. I feel yucky about it. Let's talk.* I walked downstairs, mad as hell, not even sure of what I might say, and knocked on her door. "Listen," I said after she opened it. "Racism. OK? Racism. I am trying to figure out how to survive and navigate everyday racism as a black woman in America, and you're not helping."

"You can't just barge in here," Molly said, clutching her proverbial pearls. "It's always about you, and what you want, and what you think. You just come in and take up space like you own it." I wondered if she had any idea how much she sounded like her father at this moment. The presumption that she, or any white person, could tell me how or when or where to exist.

I walked out of her mod, and back upstairs to mine. "Told you," Lottie said over the phone.

⊹ Thirty-Nine ⊹

I stood agape at the bookshelves filled with books by black writers, among them June Jordan, Alice Walker, and Toni Morrison, all personally signed over to the woman standing next to me, Michael's mother, Claudia.

Tall and elegant-looking, like her son, Claudia showed me her books as if they were precious and rare gemstones, and I held each one with the same regard. Romare Bearden and Jacob Lawrence paintings hung framed on the walls, with faded velvet upholstery in muted colors on the couch and chairs, beaded pillows, family photographs, and beautiful, ornate vases filling the room. "So you," Claudia said, her voice husky, low, and feminine, "are the woman called Rebecca."

I talked about Claudia the whole way back to Hampshire, asking Michael a flurry of questions about her life and work, prompting him to suggest, teasingly, that I was more in love with his mother than I was with him. It was true that in Claudia I saw the black mother I'd never had—literary-minded, stately, and fearless—and felt drawn to her more than any of the other, sadly few, older black women I'd been exposed to in my life. It was like pixie dust from the books I'd read at UNH with Elijah, from Toni and Zora and Audre and Alice, was sprinkled all over the shelves, and Claudia, herself glorious, erudite in the pigmentation of her flesh, was a standing wand spreading it all even further.

In my journal, after Michael and I visited his mother in Cambridge, I wrote:

I've absolutely had it with white people. I'm sorry, but Jesus, I've put my time in. Black culture is rich and it's my heritage. I'm moving to Atlanta after I graduate because I have absolutely decided that I want to be surrounded by black folks. I want to work for a black literary publication, I want to be involved with urban politics, I want to contribute to, create and encourage black culture, I want to celebrate Kwanzaa instead of Christmas. I want to start a new life that is completely my own. I choose blackness. Although I am half white and was raised in a culturally white environment, I am choosing blackness, because there is more dignity in that. I want my kids to be brown. I want my life to be brown, as I am.

That January, after another couple of months of not being in touch, Tess wrote me a letter that began, *You do not exist.* She had decided to move forward with the book idea on her own.

She went on to explain that she'd tried to request a copy of my birth certificate, but the hospital told her it was impounded—that's what they did with the birth certificates of babies put up for adoption in 1969. She wrote:

I did not birth you, you did not come from me. I am not your mother, never have been. You are not my daughter, never were. Your life began when, at 3 years old (or whenever), you were legally claimed by the Carrolls and recognized as a member of that family by the state of New Hampshire. The Third World stork brought you.

This letter, more than others, rocked me, because she wasn't attacking or judging me; she was literally erasing me from existence. I called Mom and Dad, who had been instantly against the book idea when I told them about it in July when Tess had first brought it up.

"You have to let this saga go," Dad said.

"She's trying to manipulate you," Mom said. "And she's obviously already planning to paint us in a bad light."

How was it that they were only concerned about how *they* might come across badly in a book about *my* adoption and reunion? Where had they been when I was being eaten alive by Tess and lost my entire sense of self in those early years after the reunion? Shouldn't they have been the ones to help me get that sense of self back? What happened to their scoops and buckets of love and encouragement from when I was a little girl? Surely they could see she was missing—that little girl they used to tell was special and talented and gorgeous.

A few days later, Mom sent me a letter:

> *Heard on some crappy TV channel that one of the most compelling needs is a need to belong and maybe that is what drives you toward the destructive rocks of the Bancrofts. You know you belong to us and we to you.*

Confused, hurt, angry, and sad by the rollicking mess of my relationship with Tess, I turned to Lottie, Deja, and Ruby for one of our frequent "war council" gatherings at the Umoja center, when we hashed out all that was troubling us in our lives.

"Fuck her," Lottie said about Tess and her most recent letter. "Listen, Rebecca, have her in your life, if you can, if you love her, but you can't let her destroy you like this."

"She said I didn't *exist*," I said.

"Sis, girl, what? Why? Why do you even mess with her?" Ruby said, talking out the side of her mouth, fixing herself on something else in the room, as she always did. Deja, characteristic of her, had said little, but her expression had an opinion.

"What, Deja?" I said. I could tell that she was quietly going over the ways to tell me how to do better. "Say it."

"I can't tell you shit, and you know it," Deja said, in the spoken-word cadence that was really just the way she spoke. "But why are you trying to break your own heart?"

I felt so grateful for Deja at that moment, for all three of these black women, and so truly afflicted to my core that I'd been without them, and other black girls and women, throughout my life growing up.

"What do you think your birth father would say about all this?" Michael asked tenderly, a few days later, as I wept in his arms after another volatile phone conversation with Tess, during which she told me I was flailing as a person, that I seemed misguided and listless.

I'd not thought about my birth father in this context at all, when he might have offered a distinct counterpoint to my birth mother, and of course it made sense that Michael would bring him up, as a black man who placed such a premium on the voices of black folks.

"I don't know," I said. Michael held my face in his broad, loving hands, looking straight at me. "I mean, he's still alive, isn't he? Couldn't you find out?"

At that moment, I decided that I needed to find Joe Banks before I did anything else with my life after graduation in May. Roy, who somehow knew where everyone was, like an emissary of descendants, reported that Joe had last been seen in the late '80s around the Berklee College of Music in Boston, where he couldn't afford classes but would sometimes jam with students.

Within a few months, I'd secured an internship at Blackside Productions, the film company that produced *Eyes on the Prize*, and after graduation, I was moving to Boston.

✢ Forty ✢

I found a studio apartment that I could barely afford on Hemenway Street in Boston, not far from the Fens in Back Bay, about three blocks from Berklee. Like *Mother Jones*, Blackside paid a very small stipend, and I had to hustle to make rent and other living expenses. I got a waitressing job at a popular restaurant in Harvard Square and split my time between the two, with more time waitressing than listening to archived speeches by Malcolm X.

Michael was living at home with Claudia and his stepfather, a white man named Pat, making that his home base while he tried to book poetry readings and spoken-word gigs, not sure what he wanted to do otherwise but certain he wanted to do it with me. Over Indian food one night, we talked about a wedding, and kids.

A few months before I graduated, Michael and I had gone to a conference in Paris on the subject of black expatriates, and stayed together in the garret of an apartment owned by friends of Michael's family. We went to the Sorbonne during the day and listened to speakers like Henry Louis Gates Jr., Cornel West, Barbara Chase-Riboud, and French historian Michel Fabre; ate crepes from street carts at night; and then climbed the steep staircase up to our little room above an apartment in the sixth arrondissement of Paris and fucked our brains out.

When we got back to Hampshire, I took a pregnancy test and

it came back positive. Michael, whose face lit up like a Christmas tree when I told him I was pregnant, deferred to me entirely on how I wanted to handle the pregnancy. I was twenty-two years old, and did not for one minute hesitate about whether I would have an abortion. It was my choice, free and easy at the Planned Parenthood off campus.

Now, as we finished up our chicken masala, naan, and yellow curry, we talked dreamily about our future together. We envisioned a big tent outside, at night, with tiki lights and white tablecloths, giant bouquets of wildflowers in plum and red colors in the center of each table, cream-colored streamers hanging from tent pole to tent pole, and piles of marvelous food. Our fairy-tale wedding would extend to a honeymoon back in Paris, near where we had stayed in February for the conference, where we would eat crepes in the street and think about names from Toni Morrison novels for our children.

A few weeks before graduation, I cut all my hair off, and if I was going to keep it this short, I'd need someone who knew how to manage black hair to maintain it. Which was how I found myself sitting in a barber chair at Ace Studio on a hot afternoon in August.

Ace Studio was a barbershop on Massachusetts Avenue that I passed on my way to Blackside from my apartment on Hemenway Street, and there were always young black men hanging out in front, laughing and getting up, being foolish and funny. I could hear them from fifty feet away, and always smiled as I passed, flirty and curious, but had never stopped before when they'd shout, "Hey, sis! Come through, girl!"

"Whatchu doin' in here, girl," said Jaden, the young and cocky one who'd been hollering at me.

"I just need a cleanup," I said.

"Oh, you need a *cleanup*," Jaden said, mocking me.

"Yeah, can you do it?" I said, with a bit of an attitude now. I had moved to Boston to find my black birth father, with my black boyfriend, and was doing an internship at one of the blackest documentary film production companies in America, so go ahead and try me, Black Man.

"Yeah, sure," he said, his smile spreading across his face and down into his body.

Michael and I had been apart for several days while he toured with his band when I invited him to meet me at a tea house in Harvard Square. I'd grown restless and concerned that our relationship was turning into a friendship. There was so much love between us, but our conversations over the phone just in the days when he was away had lost their spark. And if I was being perfectly honest, even before the dinner over Indian food when we'd talked about marriage, things between us had felt more comfortable than thrilling and vital, as it was in the beginning.

"Are you breaking up with me? Is this because I've been away?" Michael said. He'd successfully booked gigs that had taken him out of town for the first chunk of the summer, and we hadn't seen each other, or been intimate, for weeks.

"I just feel disengaged," I said.

That was the absolute truth of how I felt, and we had always been bracingly honest with each other. Michael looked at me, took a sip of his tea, and gave way to acceptance, and sadness.

"I love you," he said.

"I love you, too," I said.

It wasn't as cliché as actually saying to each other that we'd stay friends, but we both knew we would, and we are to this day. He's been sober for twenty years.

✛ ✛

I didn't break up with Michael to date Jaden, but there was a clear attraction, and the next time I went in for a cleanup, a couple weeks later, he asked me to dinner, and pretty soon after, we were seeing each other regularly. Slight and boyish, with sea green eyes and scalp-short hair, Jaden told me he was second-generation Cape Verdean. He had a quick temper, and saw me as an opportunity more than a girlfriend. He wanted more for himself than the barbershop, he told me, and I had "that white education and shit." We both wanted something from each other we thought we could get by osmosis. I thought I could get blacker, and he thought he could get smarter, the lack of nuance in our singular endeavors lost on us both.

"See, girl, this is what white girls have over you all, they know how to take care of themselves," Jaden said one night, pinching my belly fat after we'd just had sex.

"That's really rude," I said.

He pinched my belly harder. "What's wrong with you? You want a fat lip? I'm trying to tell you something about yourself. I'm just saying, honey," he said, trying to sound sweet now. He'd never hit me, but he'd threatened more than once. "You have a good body, I wouldn't be with you if you didn't. But this is one of them things that white women got over on black women. They know how to take care of themselves."

The truth is, I agreed with him. Had I not starved myself off and on throughout my entire life to make my body look like those of the white women who "know how to take care of themselves"? I was reminded of what Wyatt said about Sophie when we first met, how she didn't take care of herself, meaning that she was overweight. It was astonishing how quickly and easily I could revert back to white standards of beauty.

Elsa was who I turned to the most about my relationship with Jaden, which, not surprisingly, unraveled fast. She and I had become good friends as soon as I started working at Blackside, where she was a producer. A black woman who had gone to mostly all-white schools, Elsa understood what it felt like to navigate white spaces as the only black person. She was the latest in a series of black friends, mentors, or boyfriends (whom I'd started to think were sent by the ancestors) who, when I needed them the most, reassured me of the blackness I was still instinctively trying to own.

"Even though we grew up around white people," Elsa offered after I told her what Jaden had said about my body, and how I didn't know why I stayed with him, "we still feel the need to take care of our men, right?"

"Yes! I thought I couldn't claim that, but I feel it, I really do, like in a soulful way," I said. We were sitting in the coffee room at Blackside, taking a break to connect, the original promotional poster for *Eyes on the Prize* framed and mounted on the wall behind us.

"Our blackness is in us, and we are in it, all the time," she said, her eyes warm, knowing. We smiled, sighed, laughed, and went back to work. Jaden and I broke up a few months later.

☼ Forty-One ☼

I received another postcard from Tess, who had turned to examining my relationship with Dad, ostensibly as part of her book research.

> *OK. I just read a chapter in* Women and Their Fathers *by V. Secunda and I cannot get over what I read because the information on The Favored Daughter is* excruciatingly *familiar. I'm serious. Do you want me to send excerpts, do you want to get the book, do you want me to read it to you over the phone, or forget about it for now?*

I wanted none of the above. But, as usual, what I wanted remained irrelevant to her, and less than a week later, when Woody Allen released a public statement announcing that he was, in fact, in a relationship with Soon-Yi Previn, the adopted Korean daughter of his former partner, Mia Farrow, Tess sent me a letter that began: *Sound familiar? Re: Woody + Soon-yi, and you + DMC?* It felt like the sky had opened up and sucked me into an alternate universe.

"You have all the signs of being traumatized as a child," Tess said when I called her to talk about the letter, and her less-than-subtle insinuation.

Ya think? I thought to myself.

"Sexually traumatized," she clarified in response to my silence on the other end.

"OK, but why my father?"

"Because he is incapable of seeing you as his daughter," she said, firmly in her element. "I've said it all along—you are more confidante and muse than daughter to him."

"Right, but that doesn't mean he molested me."

"Think about it, Rebecca. Even if you don't remember anything specific from your early childhood, think of all the late nights with him you told me about, when you guys stayed up talking and smoking and drinking and telling each other intimate details about your relationships. Fathers and daughters don't do that."

And then, in a moment that felt like sticking a shard of glass into my neck, I thought she might be right. I did feel like something had happened to me as a child, something sexual or at the very least inappropriate—something I carried in my bones, but had no clear vision about. Dad and I were close, and we *did* have a relationship that was wildly different and separate from the relationship he had with his two other children, his biological children. I didn't believe he had molested me, but I started to think that someone else had.

"I guess I've always felt something happened in my childhood, too, but I really don't think it was my father," I said, cautiously.

"Who else would it be? The younger you were, which would account for you not remembering, the more likely it was a family member who abused you," Tess explained. "Statistically, something like 50 percent of young kids who are molested are molested by family members. You have to confront him."

What if she was right? I thought. What if I'd blocked it out? What if Dad's blurred boundaries in his marriage had extended to his daughter who wasn't his biological child?

"Frankly," Tess said, "I don't believe that most white adoptive fathers are able to see their ethnic-looking daughters as their actual daughters."

Again, I wrote a letter making extreme accusations against a man I held dear, accusations fed to me by Tess, this time addressed to both Mom and Dad. I sat on the idea of it for a day, and then another day. I didn't want to write it, but I couldn't see that Tess was trying to sabotage my relationship with Dad. And I also felt that if anyone would understand how important it was for me to reconcile myself with whatever had happened to me as a little girl—something that had shaped the way I responded to men, and sex—it was Dad.

Whether Dad was innocent or guilty, I trusted that he would respond to a claim that I tried to word as gently as possible. *I think maybe our relationship was inappropriate when I was growing up*, I wrote. *I think maybe some lines might have been crossed.*

Only Mom read it, and she was devastated.

"How could you write something like this?" Her voice trembled on the other end of the phone. "David would never do something like this, he would never hurt you, I just can't believe you would write something like this."

"Did Dad read it?"

"No, but I told him about it, and he's so hurt, Becky. So hurt. My God. And he just doesn't want to have anything to do with it."

"Something happened to me, Mom."

"Well, it wasn't something that David did, I know that for

sure," she said. "And I hope you apologize to him, or never bring this up again."

I didn't, and we all pretended the letter never happened. I regret only that Tess had forced my hand. But Dad's nonresponse changed the tenor of our relationship forever. I knew Mom was right, that he could never have hurt me, but I could hardly bear the fact that he refused to tell me that himself.

⁕ Forty-Two ⁕

The minute I walked in the door for my interview and saw Damian, it was over for me. He was sitting at a small round deuce table near the back of the café, wire-rimmed glasses resting on his forehead, looking over a food order, his velvet ebony-black skin emitting a near torrent of magnetism. I swear my knees buckled. Damian was the chef and co-owner of a new black-owned restaurant, Take It Black, along with his brother Clive.

Blackside didn't have enough funding to keep me on as a full-time production assistant, and I wasn't making enough money as a waitress to keep my studio apartment on Hemenway Street. I moved in with Monique, my best friend from a year of scooping ice cream during high school, and her boyfriend from college, Marco, a fun-loving guy from a working-class Italian American family in Revere, Massachusetts.

When I started at Take It Black, Damian was dating a thin white woman named Meg with long blonde hair and the annoying energy of a sprite. Meg came into the restaurant often, usually right at closing time, and I hated her. Damian's ex-girlfriend Rachel, also white, also often showed up at the restaurant. When Rachel came, she and Damian would sit at a table going over what looked like paperwork. It never occurred to me that Rachel might be an investor in the restaurant, which it turned out she was.

Take It Black was more a café than a full-blown restaurant, vibrant and cozy, with orange walls and big glass windows. It seated about twenty-five customers, and most evening shifts I worked the entire floor, while Damian cooked and Clive managed the floor and register, handling the after-dinner cappuccino and latte orders. Sometimes their younger brother Zachary came to help out as a dishwasher.

Damian and Clive came from a family of seven children whose parents immigrated to the States from the West Indies when they were kids. Damian was not the oldest, but was by far the most charismatic and ambitious, and he knew it. He and Clive were both obsessed with style and luxury goods—both drove BMWs and collected antique Bulova watches. They smoked expensive cigars and shopped at high-end fashion boutiques like Alan Bilzerian and the now closed Louis of Boston.

When I met him, I was heavier than I'd been in a long time, and my hair was in between lengths. I hated what I saw when I looked in the mirror. But even if I wasn't feeling confident about my appearance, I felt an absolute, undeniable sense of urgency to pursue Damian aggressively.

I asked him out several times, just as friends, I said, because I knew he was with Meg, and he finally agreed to see a play with me in the South End of Boston, not far from the Blackside offices, that was written and directed by a young black woman playwright.

As soon as the theater went dark and the stage lights went up, we inched closer toward each other, and it felt less like we were watching a play and more as if we had settled into the bucket seat of a Ferris wheel just before it started to rise and swing. He put his arm around me and kissed me behind my ear, while I pretended to watch the play. We left at intermission and ran through the streets holding hands, looking for a place to get something to eat, but mostly flying high in this sudden, preternatural fantasy-like feeling between us.

Damian loved a fancy restaurant, and we landed at a newly opened spot on Newbury Street, where he ordered a Bombay Sapphire on the rocks, and I had a glass of chardonnay, and then another, and another. We weren't stumbling drunk when we left the restaurant—we were already love-drunk, and the alcohol was just trying to catch up.

It was well past eleven when we got back to my apartment. Monique and Marco were asleep. In the spare bedroom of Monique's basement apartment that I'd made my own, Damian ran his hands over my body and murmured words that sounded like testimonial. "This is what I want," he whispered. "It's like a Spike Lee movie."

Things got very intense, very quickly between me and Damian. It was love at first sight for me, and while Damian told me he'd broken things off with Meg and that it was just me now, I knew that likely wasn't the entire truth. He also worked constantly. The restaurant was new, and he was the chef and co-owner, which meant long hours into the night and few days off. Most of the time I would meet him at the bar of a swanky restaurant in the Back Bay or South End of Boston at about nine or ten o'clock, after he'd fired his last oven-roasted, gourmet pizza with arugula and Asiago cheese.

Our go-to spot was the Cottonwood Cafe, an upscale Southwestern restaurant, now defunct, known for its enchiladas and margaritas. It had a long, roomy cottonwood bar where you could drink and eat. Damian never wanted to sit at an actual table when we went out; he liked both the exposure and intimacy of a bar.

Before Damian and I started seeing each other, I was never much of a drinker. The first time I got drunk was in high school, like it is for most people, when I drank three beers at a party and the room began to spin. I hated the feeling, and though I continued to occasionally drink socially throughout high school and college, it wasn't a regular thing for me. When I was with Damian, drinking intensified my already frighteningly ardent and intoxicating feelings for him, and whatever I could do to hold onto them longer, or to feel them in a bigger way, I gave in to. Damian was also in the restaurant business, where drinking comes with the territory, and it became part of our culture as a couple.

My drink was chardonnay—I couldn't handle hard liquor, and my palate was not yet sophisticated enough for red wine. The sugary taste of it appealed to my childlike sweet tooth, although it wasn't really about the taste so much as the high that two glasses would give me, when I would imagine the faces of our brown babies in Damian's mahogany-brown face.

We had been formally together for less than a month when the pregnancy test came back positive—again. I'd gotten pregnant that first night we were together, after we left the play at intermission.

Wyatt and I had been diligent about birth control, or rather *I* had been diligent about birth control. After the diaphragm that Tess took me to get, which felt messy and inconvenient when I started having regular sex, I went on two different prescriptions of the Pill, both of which had horrible side effects, and tried the sponge, also terrible. Michael and I weren't consistent, clearly, although Jaden and I were, but with Damian, not at all. In fact, we never once even had a conversation about birth control.

I'd been chain-smoking all day before Damian arrived, and hadn't eaten for hours. We barely knew each other, but I couldn't imagine my life without him. I felt weak and vulnerable in his arms as he rocked me and gingerly questioned my choice.

"You could give the baby up for adoption," he said obtusely. I didn't tell Damian that I could not possibly give a child up for adoption after what I'd gone through with my own, or that I'd had one abortion already. "Or you could keep it." He never said "we." I laid my head on Damian's shoulder, and remembered the night we were first together, when he whispered in my ear, "Imagine this is ten years from now," his voice low and liquid, dripping down the back of my neck. "We'd be making love to make a baby."

But I wasn't ready. I wanted to have a baby, and I wanted to have a baby with Damian, but I knew in my gut, as with my first pregnancy, that I wasn't ready. Because what if I didn't have the courage after the baby was born to keep it?

Throngs of picketers held signs with pictures of dead babies and shouted "Murderer!" outside the Planned Parenthood in Boston, and my friend Monique sheltered me with her body as she pushed our way through to the clinic entrance, then sat in the waiting room until it was over. I remembered how much I loved her as I cried in her arms, comforted by the honey smell of her hair and the soothing, melodic sound of her voice. "It's OK," she whispered. "You haven't done anything wrong."

Forty-Three

My college thesis project was a collection of narrative interviews with four black women writers, three of whom were also professors in the Pioneer Valley, where Hampshire was located, and whom I chose largely out of convenience. But the best interview was with a woman I met in Paris, at the conference Michael and I went to in the winter of my last semester. Her name was Davida, and she was funny and electric, self-possessed and brilliant. I thought I'd be able to sell a book about what it meant to be a black woman writer on her interview alone.

The genre of interviewing I developed in college was part Studs Terkel, the white Chicago-based oral historian whose 1992 book, *Race*, had been a major influence for me when I was researching my thesis, and part oral tradition of both African and black American cultures, much of which was inspired by Michael. After I interviewed a subject, I edited out my voice and wove the answers together to create a seamless, single-voice narrative. For my thesis, I introduced the collection by explaining its connection to Audre Lorde and her essay "Uses of the Erotic," in which she describes the erotic as a resource, the sense of balance between our sense of self and the chaos of our strongest feelings.

Dad had a literary agent in New York named Lila, who had sold his trilogy of natural history books. Her client list wasn't an exact fit for me, but Dad encouraged me to send her my idea for a book I wanted to write. In my query letter to Lila, I included my college thesis, which was to celebrate the unique culture made by black women who work with words, use them as a resource, and weave their womanness, their blackness, in and out and around those words. Lila called the day she received my package, and offered to represent me on the spot. A few weeks later, she sold the proposal to Random House, a major publishing house, for $20,000, which felt like winning the lottery to me.

That year, three books by black women writers were all on the *New York Times* best sellers list at the same time, for the first time in history—*Jazz*, by Toni Morrison; *Waiting to Exhale*, by Terry Mc-Millan; and *Possessing the Secret of Joy*, by Alice Walker. It was a good time to be a black woman writer, and I was glad to have had the foresight to see it coming.

I wanted to have similar success, and I threw myself into interviews for the book, which was due to my publisher in a year. I scheduled my interviews on days off from the restaurant if I needed to travel, but also did a handful of interviews over the phone. The book included writers who were well-known, like Rita Dove, June Jordan, and Gloria Naylor, and others who were just starting out, like Davida.

The first batch of letters I sent out were to Toni Morrison, Terry McMillan, and Alice Walker, none of whom responded. I reached out to other high-profile writers, too, among them Maya Angelou, Toni Cade Bambara, and, of course, my original inspiration, Audre Lorde, who was gravely ill at the time and died of breast cancer that November.

"When I write essays I always try to keep in mind a hypothetical adversary I am trying to convert into an ally or a comrade," June Jordan told me, at her home in Berkeley, California. Jordan, who attributed her emergence as a poet and activist to the lack of black writers and voices presented to her at a private high school and college she attended, may have been the interview that stayed with me the most, after Davida's.

"I write essays to galvanize my folks, whoever they are, to go and kill somebody, you know, something like that." She was rousing and unfaltering, vulnerable and stoic, with a short graying afro, perfectly straight teeth, and cinnamon skin.

I titled the book *I Know What the Red Clay Looks Like*, as a nod to the red clay in Georgia, widely regarded in America for its richness in color and texture, which is how I felt about black women writers, and after delivering the final manuscript in the summer, I applied for a job as a front desk receptionist at Harvard's Department of Afro-American Studies. The Afro-Am department's burgeoning "dream team" was making national headlines, and led by professor and public intellectual Henry Louis "Skip" Gates Jr., whom I'd seen speaking at the same conference in Paris where I'd met Davida.

I started in August, a few months after I turned twenty-five, finished my first book, and was newly contracted to write a companion volume to *Red Clay*, with black men writers. I was the first person to greet anyone who came into the department, my desk front and center as soon as you walked in the door, and it was a busy, popular department. Students and teachers came in and out all day long, journalists and filmmakers would come to interview Skip, and various speakers came to give lectures as part of the colloquium series Skip had established and named after W. E. B. Du Bois.

The department also served as the office for *Transition* magazine, the celebrated journal covering arts, politics, and culture from the African Diaspora and, at the time, edited by Henry Finder, who was the first editor to read my personal writing before getting the call of a lifetime to become an editor at *The New Yorker*.

"Of course it's good," Henry said when I showed him the start of a short essay called "Soul Notes," riffing loosely on Baldwin's *Notes of a Native Son*. I was trying to understand my identity through Baldwin's lens, and it felt like I didn't know what I was doing.

"It would be better to start with your own story, not Baldwin's," Henry said.

"But is it any good?" I asked.

"I wouldn't be giving you feedback if it wasn't."

I answered the phones and sorted the mail, but I made the position at the Department of Afro-American Studies into something that was less customer service and more master of ceremonies. Whatever drama there was going on with Damian, I loved going to my job every day. Then, early in September, a senior student named Caryn came in for her first class of the semester.

Caryn exuded an indefectible, humor-rich spirit. She wasn't just funny; she lived inside her laughter, frank and lyrical, and invited everyone else to join her there. While Jazmine, Kevin's sister, whom I bonded with during our high school trip to Washington, DC, was ultra cool, and Lottie, Deja, and Ruby from Hampshire were excellent girlfriends, Caryn felt like home. Like the feeling that your heart will go on beating, every sound you hear is safe and familiar, and every time you return after you've left, you'll know, proudly and rightly, that you have grown, but that you are always welcome.

"You should really go natural," I said, looking at her straightened perm one afternoon about two weeks after we'd met, when she'd paused to stop at my desk before class, as she always did.

"I really want to, but I'm not ready," she said, as if picking up a conversation midway through, even though we'd never talked about hair before. "I'll tell you what, though, sis. You better put some oil in your hair. All that free, natural hair of yours, all your baby hairs are *pleading* with you, Rebecca, *pleading*, 'Mommy, please give us some oil, *please*, just a little!'"

"I don't know how to do it myself!" I bemoaned, through laughter.

"I see the hippie white people who raised you didn't know either," she said, laughing along,

Caryn was graduating from Harvard in June, and we started talking about where she might move, what kind of job she'd be looking for. We talked about how great it would be if we could move somewhere together—we both thought New York would be a dream.

∻ Forty-Four ∻

*D*amian *lived in a three-story house* with his brother Clive not far from the restaurant, where he had a claw-foot tub in his bedroom, and would soak in bath salts and smoke a cigar most nights after work, his arms glistening as he rested them on each side. I'd sit across from him on an expensive divan that he somehow had the money to buy, and try to get him to talk about things like the Rodney King trial or Angela Bassett's performance as Tina Turner in the film *What's Love Got to Do with It*, which we saw together and I *loved*. Damian seldom expressed a particular political opinion or view, and it seemed as if he'd only just begun to think about race or his own racial identity when he met me.

Damian's personal aesthetic was largely inspired, he told me, by Sting, whose 1993 album, *Ten Summoner's Tales*, could well have been the soundtrack to our relationship it was playing so often in Damian's car. His style was bohemian chic, more Lenny Kravitz than Will Smith, although he never referenced either of those men, or any black male role models. It felt like I was trying to shed the influence of whiteness, while Damian was trying to build on it, and I wondered if it was possible to reverse engineer your racial identity.

Everything he told me about his life after immigrating to the States as a young boy included the power and influence of a white person.

Damian said that he'd met his ex Rachel when he was nineteen years old and didn't know anything about anything, much less nice clothes and good food, expensive cars. He said Rachel, who was older and from a wealthy Jewish family, had introduced him to all of that, taught him good taste. Instinctively, I found this disturbing on a number of levels, but it was a dynamic that I also felt some measure of compassion toward. I liked nice things, too, although I'd been drawn to them on my own from a very early age, and had started working so that I could afford to buy them as soon as I was old enough to babysit. Was there something inherently white about having a particular kind of good taste? Did it make Damian and me less black because we liked lattes and scones?

As usual, I tried to work things out through writing, and in my journal wrote:

Damian has a very serious black complex, and I do believe that the part of me he feels attracted to is my whiteness. But see I am really beyond that. I can't stay with someone who triggers my self-doubt, who doesn't love his blackness. . . . Damian doesn't realize that his white aspirations make him look like a fool—people are laughing at him. Both black folks and white folks. He hates his blackness so much he needs to shop at Barney's. He needs to eat at fancy restaurants. He needed Rachel's white money to launch his career. He has to come to terms with his blackness and mine. He needs to like his nappy hair.

One night after work at Harvard, I walked into the restaurant wearing a sweatshirt I'd borrowed from Damian, who was talking with Rachel over the counter. Tall with brown hair and bangs, eyes fragile and protective, Rachel looked at me like I'd stolen something of hers.

"You have to tell me, Damian, I'm serious. Is there still

something going on with you two?" I said after Rachel stormed off. It was near closing time and the restaurant was quiet.

"Beck, how many times do we have to have this conversation? How many times do I have to tell you that there is *nothing* going on between me and Rachel?" Damian turned away. "I have to close up, do you want to wait or not?"

A few days later, I'd been home from work for less than an hour when the doorbell rang. I could look out the window to see who was at the door, and when I made out the silhouette of Rachel standing under the porch light, my stomach sank. How did she know where I lived?

"That sweatshirt you were wearing," she said, towering over me in the doorway, cool autumn air spilling in from behind her. "It's mine. That sweatshirt belongs to me."

"Oh," I said, confused and offended that she'd felt the need to come to my home uninvited to tell me this. "OK."

"And also," she said, rattled, "I don't know why you're so rude to me when I'm in the restaurant, especially now, because of the baby."

"I'm sorry, what?" Rachel had been wearing an oversized jacket at the restaurant that night, but now that she was in a more fitted wool sweater, I could see the bump just starting to show. Rachel was six months pregnant with Damian's baby. I felt like I was going to throw up, and grabbed onto the door to keep myself steady.

"You didn't know?"

"Damian and I have been together for ten months! No, I didn't know!" I shouted, trying not to lose it completely.

"Oh," she said, looking hurt, as if *she* were the victim here. "He told me it wasn't that serious with you."

"You need to leave," I said.

After I shut the door behind her, I fell apart. Heaving and

moaning and crying. I couldn't believe this was happening. After I managed to pull myself together, I was enraged.

Damian and I had plans to meet up later that night. When I didn't show up for our plans to meet, the phone started ringing nonstop. I let him keep calling three or four times before finally picking up.

"I know about the baby," I said, absolutely seething.

"What baby?"

"Rachel's baby."

"Listen, Beck, I can explain. It wasn't like that."

I almost laughed out loud at the irony of a Spike Lee reference popping into my brain—Mars Blackmon's incessant "Please, baby—please, baby—baby baby, please" when he's begging Nola not to break up with him in *She's Gotta Have It*—given that Damian had said on our first night together that the two of us in a dark basement bedroom, half dressed, was like a scene from a Spike Lee movie.

"Don't call me again," I said, and hung up. In my gut, I knew all along that he'd been cheating, and he had not only lied when I asked, but gaslit me every single time as well.

✢ Forty-Five ✢

I rubbed my thumbs over the two pictures inside my jacket pocket as Roy and I walked through Harvard Square to the Au Bon Pain on the other side. I brought them in case I didn't recognize my birth father right away, although I was sure I would. I was anxious, wrecked from the break with Damian, and stunned by Roy's call out of the blue telling me he'd found Joe and set up a time for us to meet. I'd been in Boston for a year, and this was the first time Roy had contacted me with any kind of lead.

Past a certain hour, that Au Bon Pain in Harvard Square stopped being the quick drop-in spot for a halfway decent croissant and began its evening run as a gathering spot for the homeless, who nursed cold coffees and, if they were lucky, nibbled on day-old pastries that hadn't sold during the morning rush. Roy and I stood inside, where the ceiling-wide fluorescent lights gave the feel of a sleazy all-night diner.

Three black men sat together at one table, all wearing soiled, shabby coats and natty fingerless gloves, chatting in fellowship. I searched their faces until one of the men noticed me staring. His eyes were rheumy and bloodshot, skin dark and slick with sweat, gray sprigs of different-length hair popping out from under a holey wool cap. I looked away, embarrassed by the judgment I felt toward him. My birth father was not among these men, and after twenty minutes, it was clear he wasn't coming.

"I'm sure he just got his wires crossed," Roy said, trying to reassure me. "I'll try him again. It's hard to get through to him. You know, he doesn't have a phone, that's why I had to call him on the Salvation Army pay phone."

"He doesn't *live* at the Salvation Army, does he?" I asked. I hoped that my birth father wasn't homeless—that would maybe be too much for me to handle.

"I don't know if he lives there full-time, but you know, better than living among the bourgeoisie!" Roy said, trying to lighten things up and failing. "Let's go."

"That's OK," I said to Roy. "You go. I'll take the train back to Boston."

I took the pictures out of my pocket and looked at them. The meeting date had materialized so quickly that it didn't even feel like he'd stood me up. I hadn't had time to expect him, or anticipate him, after years of wondering about him, which is different.

Roy gave my shoulder an awkward pat, and I watched him as he crossed a dark Massachusetts Avenue, passed the wrought iron gates that lined Harvard University, over the cobblestone sidewalk, through the night toward his family.

A week later, Roy scheduled the meeting, same place. This time I left the pictures at home. I was feeling a different kind of anxiety as Roy and I waited at a table in the back of Au Bon Pain, facing the entrance, while the clock ticked. I was worried that Tess might have been right. That my birth father was "a dog" who wouldn't follow through. I'd told her about the first meeting when he didn't show up. "I hate to say I told you so," she said. I let her know we'd rescheduled. "Good luck with that, and please don't tell him anything about me if he does show up this time," she shot over the phone. "I don't want anything to do with it."

"There he is," Roy said.

My first thought when I looked at the man who had walked through the entrance was, *This can't possibly be the same man from the two pictures I had of my birth father.* Where were the chiseled cheekbones? The gabardine suits or even the slick safari-style jacket? The tight, cropped afro, broad shoulders, and long, lean legs? This man now rushing toward us was chubby, wearing a holey red tracksuit and eyeglasses with matching red frames, with an unkempt afro, face drenched in sweat. Roy said a loud and jovial hello, and Joe murmured hello back from the side of his face, unable to take his eyes off me, as if he were looking at something more astonishing than if the seven natural wonders of the world were suddenly lined up, side by side, each right next to the other.

I stood to greet him in a thick fog of cognitive dissonance. Joe hugged me, stood back, studied my face, tears welling, and then hugged me again. Roy left us alone to talk.

"This is why God put me on the earth," Joe said, his hands on my shoulders. "You are so beautiful. You are the reason I'm alive."

God? What? We sat down, across from each other at the table where I'd been waiting, and a strange wave of grief passed through me. I didn't know what I was mourning.

"You know, they took you from me," he said, shaken and emotional. "Tess and her mother and Roy, they took you, just like slave times. I wanted to keep you. I would have raised you on my own, but they shut me out and stole you away from me."

"But what happened with you and Tess?" I couldn't get to the idea of him raising me on his own.

"I loved her, I did. But her mother didn't like me," Joe said. "Her mother was a racist, thought she and Tess and them were better than me, so they shut me out."

Joe told me that it had felt especially important to be in my life because his own biological mother, Blanche Calloway, jazz singer and older sister to the better-known jazz singer and bandleader Cab Calloway, had no other choice but to give him up at birth, so that she could focus on her budding career. "It was hard enough for a black woman to even have a career back then," Joe said. "She couldn't have had a career and raised a child, too. I don't know who my father was, so she would have been alone, too."

I learned that Joe grew up in and out of foster care, without any lasting familial bonds or friendships, and knew of no other existing biological relatives that he might have. "I hope you'll let me see you," he said. "And that you'll call me Pops."

It was a lot to process, but I felt an unexpected affection swelling inside of me. He wasn't what I'd thought he would be, or look like I'd imagined he would. But he was gentle and vulnerable. He showed up and wanted to be in my life. I didn't know how to manage one more parent in my already cramped carousel of parents, but I knew I wanted to try.

Forty-Six

*J*ust *before Christmas, I reached out* to Joe at the number he'd given me to invite him to a Middle Eastern restaurant that played live music in Central Square so he could meet my boyfriend. Damian had begged my forgiveness, and I had acquiesced. We were trying to make things work between us. And also, after meeting Joe, I wanted to show him that I had found the blackness I'd been robbed of while growing up in the white family that adopted me.

Damian and I arrived first, and for a minute I thought Joe might not show up, but then there he was. Now that the weather was colder, he was bundled up in a sheepskin coat with shearling around the collar, the same kind of material Catherine used to make her hats with when I was growing up, and a brown wool hat, with leather gloves, no glasses. He was carrying a tote bag with various-sized objects poking out from inside.

I introduced Joe to Damian. The two locked eyes and shook hands; Damian put his other hand on top of their handshake, as if to signal some kind of assurance or mutual understanding that they could both be my protectors. Joe joined us at a table.

"I love this place!" Joe said after he gave me a hearty hug. The place was dimly lit, with a live local jazz band playing in the background.

"What do you have in the bag there, Joe?" Damian said. "Do you have something in there for me?"

Damian's way of disarming people was to play at being devilish, in an almost childlike way.

"As a matter of fact, I do!" Joe chimed, delighted to have come bearing gifts, even though I knew, because he had told me during our first conversation that he lived on welfare, that he likely could not afford them. He pulled out one clumsily wrapped gift after another, grinning the whole time. A pair of shiny silver candle-holders for me and Damian to share, a coffee mug for Damian, and a fuzzy white knit scarf especially for me that I put on right away. Damian ordered us all some food, and we talked, but mostly just ate and listened to the music, feeling like a family.

A couple of months later, Joe met me at Damian's restaurant to see where my boyfriend plied his trade. Late on a Sunday, it was in the middle of the brunch rush, but Damian saved us a corner table in front of the window, where you could see the frost begin to melt from the glare of the sun. Joe had on the same sheepskin coat and brown wool hat from our Christmas visit and carried the same tote, this time filled with a few slim, pamphlet-like books sticking out.

Joe appeared less relaxed than he'd been in December, and kept his coat and hat on, as if prepared to make a quick exit if necessary. He flipped through the pages in one of the books, an illustrated paperback that looked self-published by whoever the author was, and that featured drawings of all the white men throughout history who were actually black. "They had to pass, you see," Joe said, pointing to a man who looked like George Washington, but whose name I forget. "Because America hates black men," he said, the expression on his face turning suddenly anxious. "In fact, the government's been watching me for twenty years."

Joe told me he was suing the government for emotional distress, and was seeking thousands of dollars in damages. I was grateful to have my birth father in my life, even if I wasn't quite ready to call him Pops, as he'd asked me to, but I definitely wasn't ready for his paranoia—for one, because mental health issues run in the family on Tess's side, and the older I got, the more I lived in constant fear that one morning I would wake up to discover I was schizophrenic, like Tess's mother, Lena. If Joe was also schizophrenic or mentally ill, which I was only speculating about based on his behavior, then I would for sure be, too, I thought.

A month later, I called Joe to tell him that I was moving to New York with one of my best friends, Caryn, and that I got a coveted job at a fancy magazine.

"You'll stay in touch with me, now, won't you?" he said over the phone.

I pictured him leaning against the wall next to a hall phone at the Salvation Army in Central Square, where he did live most of the time.

"I will. Take care, Pops," I said, and hung up.

✢ Forty-Seven ✢

I don't know why I agreed to write the afterword for Tess's book about us. The one I couldn't bring myself to even read. I also granted her permission to use my name and publish a few of my letters to her, and agreed to do press after publication, without which, her agent told her, she wouldn't have had a deal. Or at the very least, a much smaller advance.

Even after thirteen fraught years, during which I had felt crushed and judged by Tess at nearly every turn, I didn't wish her any ill will. We had a very complicated relationship, I reasoned, which was also extraordinary. I was an adult now, and an aspiring writer myself. I could be gracious enough to help her share our story without having to go in all the way—a story that very well might, as she had suggested, help other people trying to navigate the emotionally turbulent maze of adoption and reunion.

In my first draft of the afterword, I tried to tackle the subject of adoption from an objective point of view, which was naive, but also such a clear indication that I wasn't ready to write about it from a personal place.

Tess sent the following notes back:

I'm thinking you may not be an "issues" writer—or that you're just not old enough to be one. Essayists are at their best, and the best in history,

are all firmly middle-aged and over (G. B. Shaw, D. Parker, etc.). Sitting
back and opining is very hard to do while still in the grip of growing
and self-actualization, tho, ironically, an intrinsic part of it.

After that, I surrendered to her, another successful coup of hers in what continued to feel like an endless war of attrition between us, and agreed to a heavily edited afterword. I still couldn't bring myself to read the manuscript all the way through, and moved to New York wishing I could just forget about it and focus instead on my new job and life, and the publication of my own book, *I Know What the Red Clay Looks Like*, in the coming fall.

A few months later, after I'd said goodbye to Joe, and Damian, too, and settled in New York with Caryn, my book was published to some acclaim—Whoopi Goldberg gave a blurb, saying she found its "eloquent elegance breathtaking," and Skip Gates called it "a stunning achievement"—but I was more depressed than I'd ever been in my life, and could barely enjoy its success.

At *Elle*, where I'd been hired as an editorial assistant, surrounded by near replicas of the pretty, thin white girls I'd been tormented by throughout my life, I felt inadequate both in terms of how I looked and what I hoped I could bring to the table. Who knew there was such a thing called imposter syndrome? I certainly didn't, and so continued to feel like I simply didn't deserve to be at such a high-profile, mainstream publication.

I did, though, push hard for coverage of black women in the magazine, and wrote short pieces on Edwidge Danticat, Thandie Newton, and Jada Pinkett, and did a feature-length Q&A spread with bell hooks, but I felt unwelcome and unseen. Like the editors I worked with at *Mother Jones* (other than Kim, who was black and had hired me for the internship), my editors at *Elle* were all white.

Unlike my *Mother Jones* editors, though, my *Elle* editors weren't especially interested in mentoring or helping me grow, speeding through edits and then rewriting the piece themselves rather than showing me how to be a better writer.

"This is not working," one editor said, about the piece on Danticat, a black woman author, a subject I felt reasonably confident about.

"What do you mean?" I admit to being defensive, but I also genuinely wanted to know what wasn't working—I wanted to learn.

"I don't have time to explain, I'll just fix it myself." This stung, not least of all because it was so dismissive, but also because of the implication that I couldn't write.

The magazine ran an excerpt from my book in the fall issue, but then treated me like an afterthought in the office. I knew that starting out in the magazine industry would be challenging, and that I'd need to put in my time, but this was Sisyphean. It seemed obvious to me that white women with the same title and position as I were given more bylines, and editors went to them with story ideas first.

I pitched *Mother Jones* an interview with the poet and writer Ntozake Shange, and they accepted. I had read *For Colored Girls Who Have Considered Suicide / When the Rainbow Is Enuf* some years before, but revisited it as I slipped deeper into depression. Although Ntozake had a new novel out, *Liliane*, which I used as the peg for the pitch, it was *For Colored Girls* that resonated with me the most at the time, because when I stepped outside of myself, it looked like I might be dancing around the idea of suicide myself.

I'd published a companion volume to my first book, *Swing Low*, with black men writers, which went entirely under the radar, particularly as it coincided with the publication of Tess's book. But I'd also sold the proposal for a third book, another collection of interviews, this one about the experiences of young black girls in America called *Sugar in the Raw*.

I took the train from Penn Station to the 30th Street Station in Philadelphia, where Ntozake then lived. She greeted me at the door with her long, multicolored braids and divine smile, welcoming me inside after giving me a warm hug. Inside, her house was crowded with art and books, ashtrays everywhere, and she lit one cigarette after another as she showed me around her modest-sized home. The smoke from incense and cigarettes lingered around us, colliding with the smells of aloe plants, chamomile tea, and lentils cooking in the kitchen.

We settled in on the couch to talk, and Ntozake's voice was low and raspy as her answers flew out of her mouth like carrier pigeons. I felt honored to be in her presence, but she also felt kindred. For a period after that, she would call just to talk, sometimes late at night, and we would reflect on our lives, the different generations of black women we embodied, and how to stay sane. In our interview for *Mother Jones*, she'd given an answer that resounded in my head over and over again: "I write for young girls of color, for girls who don't even exist yet, so that there is something there for them when they arrive. I can only change how they live, not how they think."

This was the answer, the line of thinking, that inspired me to ask her to write the foreword to *Sugar in the Raw*, which she agreed to immediately.

Forty-Eight

*U*nder the hot lights on the live set of *Good Morning America*, Joan Lunden asked me and Tess how we felt our relationship was now that it had been fifteen years since our reunion, and Tess had published her book.

"And what does it feel like to be a black woman, adopted by white parents, with one white biological parent as well?" Lunden asked.

"Well," I said, "I think being black and exploring my racial identity has been challenging. But it's what I write about now, and I'm committed to helping and mentoring other black girls who might be struggling with their identity."

I hadn't actually read Tess's book, but Caryn had.

"Girl, this woman hurt *my* feelings. And I don't even *know* her. Rebecca, girl. Whew," Caryn said, truly anguished as she padded her slippered feet into the kitchen, shaking her head the whole way, the gorgeous round globe of her natural crop cut slowly swaying left to right.

I knew that if I personally read whatever sequence of words was laid out in the pages of Tess's book, it would be my undoing. As long as I didn't read it, I thought, I would be safe from utter collapse.

✦ ✦

During our *Good Morning America* spot, I felt oddly at ease, enjoying myself and giving what felt like smart answers to questions about navigating and creating a racial identity both as an interracial adoptee and in America at large. After the interview, I basked in the glow as then host Joan Lunden and her producers lauded me as "a natural" on air, although I knew that Tess was watching me, so I tried not to enjoy it too much.

Ever an apostle of celebrity lore and the New York City literary cabal, Tess took us for lunch at Elaine's after our *Good Morning America* segment. Over escargot, salads, and seltzer, Tess said, "You know, I noticed something today." I fully expected her to say that I'd hogged airtime or attention, like she had when I visited her at the safe house for black girls where she'd volunteered the prior summer. The girls and I had naturally gravitated toward one another, but when Tess and I got home that night, she reprimanded me for taking over her domain. Instead, at a round table set against a wall lined with framed photographs of Elaine's beloved regulars, authors and actors, Tess said, "I heard you refer to yourself as black."

"Yeah," I said. "Because I am.

"Listen," she said. "You came out of my body and I am white, so there's no way that you're gonna just go around calling yourself black."

The sheer arrogance of her assumption that only she could grant the permission required for me to call myself black was eviscerating, and her overt contempt toward even the *idea* of me claiming my blackness felt like a dam had broken.

Turns out, I didn't need to read even one word of Tess's book to give way to collapse. Caryn came home from work that night to find me sitting on the stairway up to our bedrooms, in the dark. I'd been counting backward from fifty, thinking every time that when I got to one, I'd find a way to kill myself and do it—a razor to the wrist, downing a whole bottle of aspirin (would that even work?), maybe drink a gallon of drain cleaner (wasn't that what killed one of the Heathers in the movie *Heathers*?). I'd gone through this countdown three times by the time Caryn got home.

"Rebecca," Caryn said, sitting down next to me on the step below. "What is going on?"

"I don't want to do this anymore," I said, as if what I meant by "this" would be obvious to her.

"Honey, what are you talking about?"

"Tess and this book, and my life, and I just feel so tired, and so dead and done."

"Rebecca," Caryn said, holding my hands in hers, forcing me to look at her and focus on what she was saying. "You have too much to do in this world to give up now. Too many books to write, children to love, and people to inspire. You need to get some help, honey."

"Help like what?" I asked because I truly did not know.

"Like a therapist, honey, someone to help you work through all of this."

Pre-Google, pre-internet, Caryn offered to poll her network of folks in the nonprofit education community to see if anyone had recommendations, and came back with a list of about three names. The first and last woman I went to, from Caryn's list, was young and pleasant, white with brown hair and glasses. She asked me a series of questions: Any recent or abrupt changes, jarring events in my life, weight gain, trouble sleeping? Check, check, check, and check. I gave her a brief history of my relationship with Tess, how it had led to her book, what she'd said recently at Elaine's, and how Caryn had encouraged me to talk with someone.

When I paused to take a breath, acutely aware that I was able to take a breath, the therapist removed her glasses and said, "Your friend did the right thing by telling you to come."

"Yeah," I said, trying to harness this strange, ethereal sense of hope. "I think she might have actually saved my life." Without my even touching on my parents, or the idea of something sexually inappropriate happening to me as a child, the therapist diagnosed me with clinical depression on the spot, and wrote me a prescription for the antidepressant Zoloft.

Within two weeks of starting to take Zoloft, I felt like a superwoman. I immediately lost ten pounds, laughed out loud for the first time in months, and felt for the first time in my entire life like I could, and would, stand up to Tess and tell her how toxic our relationship had been for me.

When she called to tell me that we'd have even more to celebrate now because Hallmark wanted to make a TV movie out of her book, I said, "Absolutely fucking not." I'd done everything I said I would do to support her book. It was over for me.

✦ Forty-Nine ✦

Feeling newly emancipated from Tess, I was thrilled when Skip Gates invited me to return to the Department of Afro-American Studies, not as a receptionist but as a W. E. B. Du Bois scholar for a year-long fellowship with an office at Harvard to use as my home base while I traveled around the country to interview black girls for my book. The appointment coincided with a small grant awarded to me by the Kellogg Foundation, to be paid out through Harvard, but it wouldn't come through for a month or more. I moved back to Boston and in with Monique, who had broken up with Marco and was working at a corporate law firm and living alone in an apartment in Jamaica Plain.

It was hard to leave New York and Caryn, who stayed on in our house on Lefferts Avenue, but I knew I'd be back, that I was meant for Brooklyn, and it for me——a bastion of rugged, urban beauty and brown faces, trees fighting to grow in the cracks of concrete, the maddening subways and the sound of bass beats blaring from cars and open windows. I was glad, though, to say goodbye to *Elle*, where the most valuable lesson I learned came from Jada Pinkett, who answered my question about the difference between an interview in *Elle* versus *Essence* like this: "*Elle* feels necessary for the game, and *Essence* feels necessary for the family."

I planned to find my own place, but for the time being, Monique and I shared a bed in her one-bedroom apartment, and not long after I'd settled in, we were both startled awake in the middle of the night by a loud outcry: "I know who it was!"

I didn't even realize it was my own voice until we were both sitting upright.

"What is it?" Monique said, shaken, clutching my arm where she sensed it was, as our eyes adjusted to the dark.

"It was John, Monique," I told her, calmly and with stunning clarity. "It was John, not my dad. I just saw it in a dream, but it wasn't a dream."

"Tell me what happened," she said.

"In the dream, I am a child sitting on John's lap, and his huge hands are all over me. On my arms, in between my legs, on my chest, squeezing my thighs. Then the dream flips to his point of view, and I'm an adult," I said, describing to Monique something I couldn't believe I hadn't realized before. "And then the point of view flips back to mine, and I see those beady eyes, like, pulsating, and that sick, perverted smile."

Right after I moved back to Boston, a couple of weeks before the dream, I did a reading and book signing at a bookstore in New Hampshire owned by friends of the family. I was newly empowered—that is, medicated—feeling almost insanely sane and hyperlucid as I greeted people and signed copies of my books. This, I thought, was what it must feel like to be on cocaine. Everything was *grand*! I finished signing one book, marking a period at the end of my name with the exaggerated flare of an author, handing it back with a grateful smile. The customer smiled back, and peeled off to make room for the next person in line.

He was taller than I remembered, but those beady eyes were unmistakable. John's shoulders were hunched with his hands drawn to his chest, carrying not a book but something else, small enough to fit inside cupped hands. All the people and sounds and books around us faded, and all the adrenaline I'd been riding high on just minutes before evaporated so completely that I felt emotionally dehydrated. His tight, wide grin bore into me like a scythe as he moved closer to the signing table and opened his hands in front of me, to reveal a tattered stub of rust-colored macramé, with one greenish-brown ceramic bead tied to the end.

"Remember when you made this for me?" he said, his mouth stuck in a crude grin, like the Joker's. "You were just a little girl, my wifey, remember?"

I tried to do something with my mouth, make words or fake a smile, but nothing came, and I just sat there, simultaneously disoriented and grounded in what felt like near-dry cement but somehow worse.

"Excuse me, sir?" the woman behind him in line said kindly. "Are you going to have a book signed?"

John moved to the side, and then sank back into the crowd. Suddenly I was signing books again, as if the whole exchange had been intercut in the room's collective imagination. I didn't see him again that night, and didn't think of him again until the dream at Monique's.

The revelation of John's sexual misconduct with me as a child was sound and certain, and it was enough. I had no interest in confronting him, although I did tell Mom, who said she had thought John was rather odd, and that this didn't seem out of the realm of possibility.

I decided to put it behind me. I couldn't take on more trauma after pushing through the last of my relationship with Tess. Instead, I dove into my work on the book.

≁ *Fifty* ≁

One of my stops for Sugar in the Raw **was at the Boys and Girls Club** in Burlington, Vermont, where I presented the project, as I did in all the cities, schools, centers, and organizations I visited, and invited girls in the audience to come talk with me after if they were interested in being interviewed for the book. I wanted the book to present as broad a range as possible of black girls growing up in America, and if I had existed in super white, rural New Hampshire, there had to be other black girls in similar New England settings. Nicole, a fierce and funny seventeen-year-old biracial girl who was not at all ambivalent about calling herself black, volunteered her story, and it ended up being one of the best interviews in the book.

After two years in South America, Ryan returned to the States, and landed in Burlington. When I mapped out my travel for *Sugar in the Raw*, I included Burlington certainly for the reason of wanting a rural New England perspective, but also because I knew Ryan was there. We'd exchanged a few letters while he was out of the country, and the tenor between us was easy and forgiving.

We met up in Burlington after my interview with Nicole, then shopped for ingredients to make tacos back at his house, where we drank wine and chopped onions and tomatoes, grated cheese and danced around the kitchen like an old married couple. He was living in a small, rustic cottage just off the busy part of Burlington, with a few plants on a mostly empty bookshelf, issues of *Outside* magazine strewn about, and a thick, round wood table with mismatched chairs in the kitchen. It smelled like sautéed jalapeños and onions, steamed brown rice and summer, as we laughed and remembered each other, marveled over the fifteen difficult and impulsive years we'd known each other, how we'd both changed and hadn't.

My hair, which I'd been wearing in a shorn afro dyed strawberry blonde for book appearances, both mine and Tess's, was newly straightened, in a pixie-like style inspired by Halle Berry's look at the time, the mid-'90s. I wasn't quite as thin as I was when Ryan told me that my being skinny was "maybe" one of the reasons he found me attractive in college and not in high school, but I was still quite thin, after losing weight as a side effect of Zoloft.

When Ryan ran his hands up around my bare thighs, slid them under the size-four tulip-cut miniskirt that I remember feeling proud to fit into, and said, "You're so beautiful," I wanted to be his kind of beautiful forever. In retrospect, this was one of those moments when Whoopi Goldberg's character from *Ghost* would have said to me, "You in danger, girl!" Because of course it was a setup. We spent forty-eight hours of bliss together, during which we decided we would give our fickle relationship another try, and that he would join me for the next leg of my travel for the book.

In the morning we agreed I would leave ahead of him, and he would meet me the following week, but he changed his mind about everything.

"You can't broker a relationship," Ryan said over the phone after I'd gotten back to Boston, turning the blame on me for luring him from Berkeley three years before. *The hell I can't*, I thought to myself. My entire existence—the adoption, the reunion, the construct of race, the co-option of my identity, the fucking foundation of America—had all been the result of a brokered relationship, with white people as the brokers and black bodies as the raw commodity. *Fuck you, Ryan.*

He was right, though. I was in survivor mode and I knew it. Years of negotiating Tess's aggressively calculating behavior while simultaneously processing Mom and Dad's passively unaffected attitudes had made me terse, argumentative, and cynical. I put up an abrasive guard that pushed back with fury and desperation, while also reaching for what?—I didn't even know for sure at that point.

Three months later Ryan called to tell me he was getting married.

"Just curious," I said. "What's she look like?" Even though I knew the answer.

"I mean, she's blonde, really athletic, blue eyes," he said. "Why? What does that have to do with anything?"

That fall, I started a teaching job at an all-girls private school outside of Boston. After spending the summer talking with young black girls across the country, I was drawn to the idea of teaching high-school-age girls, particularly black girls who found themselves in predominantly white spaces. Between my eleventh grade history class and my ninth grade English class, I had about a half dozen black students.

The fall of 1995 gave us the Million Man March to discuss and the O. J. Simpson trial to watch and debate over in my history class, while I introduced my ninth graders to *The Bluest Eye* and essays by Toni Cade Bambara. Less than a month into the school year, white parents complained to the administration that I was pushing a "black agenda" on their children, while black parents wrote me personal notes thanking me for being such a powerful role model for their daughters. I spent hours on my curriculum and syllabus, pored over readings, and corrected essays and exams, channeling Elijah as I wrote careful notes in the margins. He was still the best teacher I'd ever had.

A core group of the girls, both black and white, spent nearly every free moment they had in my classroom gathered around my desk in youthful disarray, sometimes to talk about a writing assignment or the latest episode of *90210*, other times to vent about their homework or teachers from other classes. The only other black teacher at the school taught art, and was, I soon discovered, not at all interested in disrupting the status quo. It felt like I was called into the headmistress's office at least once a week to discuss protocol, boundaries, the materials I was teaching, and the discussions I was fostering among my students.

It all sounded very familiar to Dad, who told me he'd experienced the same kind of criticism and reprimand when he was a high school teacher, pushing against the system and advocating for his students. The difference, though, was that I was fighting not just the academic system but a white supremacist system as well, which didn't occur to Dad and marked another moment, like the conversation we'd had about him not having any black friends, when it was acutely clear he didn't think about race at all.

Fifty-One

"I *don't understand why you're so mad* about Spike Lee directing this Michael Jackson video," Mom said, genuinely perplexed.

"Because Spike is like *the* Black Man," I said, fuming. "He preaches this whole thing about authenticity and walking the walk as a black man, and bringing it back to the community." Mom tilted her head, trying to follow along with what I was saying. "Michael Jackson's descent into assimilated white social behavior is just the sort of bullshit that Spike criticizes."

"Well, Beck, that's very interesting."

And I believe that Mom *did* think it was interesting, in the same way that *Masterpiece Theatre* and the fashion in *Vogue* magazine were interesting.

"You seem tense, though. It seems like this whole teaching thing has stripped you of your sense of peace in some ways," she said. "It's like it's incited this rage for social causes that I've never seen in you before."

I tended not to push Mom after she reached this point in a conversation, when she'd make a sort of sweeping, preemptive statement that stealthily dipped into her reserve of incontestable knowledge that she held about her children, stored from the fifteen years, give or take, that she'd spent focused solely on our well-being.

Still, the notion that maintaining a sense of peace meant not being angry about "social issues," i.e., race, was both preposterous and offensive. I knew, though, that trying to help her understand why it was preposterous and offensive would yield unsatisfying results, with her only getting increasingly defensive and upset, and nobody better or smarter for it. And in any event, her comment had evoked a different source of rage in me.

Over the years, my alcohol consumption had changed since I drank two glasses of chardonnay with Damian at the Cottonwood Cafe. I'd broadened my palate and switched to red, and also upped the intake considerably past two glasses a few times a week. Night sweats and insomnia were among the side effects when I first started taking Zoloft, so I'd lowered the dosage and started pairing it with two or three glasses of wine to help me sleep, sometimes more, which I understood to be a potentially dangerous combination, but it suited me and I went with it.

Dad's drink was a dry vodka martini with an olive, and while he was never a blind alcoholic, as his father had been, he imbibed heartily. Dad and I both had plenty to drink when I laid into him for not thinking enough about race and the repercussions for me as a black girl growing up in rural New Hampshire, where we lived only because it suited *him* and *his* life and wants.

It was well past dinner, maybe ten at night. Dad had done the dishes, and was sitting in the living room in front of the fireplace, where the fire had begun to die out, bright orange embers like owl eyes in the dark of night. I was sitting at the kitchen table with Mom, who drank two vodka with grapefruit drinks at cocktail hour, and then never touched another drop during dinner or before bed. She was bearing witness, as she often did, of what I think she saw as art——this emotionally charged exchange between two people she loved, who were so wildly different and yet so strikingly similar.

I kept pushing until Dad stood up from his chair in the living room, turned away from me. "We have supported you! We have backed you!" he said, as if he were a patron of the arts, and I the art. "When you wanted to meet Tess, we backed you. When you took an interest in studying blacks, black culture, we supported you!"

"You 'backed' me? You 'supported' me when I wanted to meet Tess? Parenting is not a gift! And I was *eleven* years old when you 'let' me decide whether or not I wanted to meet her, and how, really *how*, could you not see how damaging that relationship has been for me?! And 'blacks'? Really, Dad?"

"You know what I meant," Dad said, dismissively.

"Beck," Mom said quietly from across the kitchen table. "You've had an awful lot to drink. Maybe you should just go to bed." The worry in her face was eclipsed only by her desire to end this conversation.

"Why are you always defending him? He can answer for himself, Mom! My God! This whole family, our whole lives, it's all about Dad and what he wants, like the entire world revolves around Dad! It's insane!"

"Your father is tired, Beck," Mom said. "It's late, come on now, let's just go to bed."

It occurred to me, maybe for the first time, that the reason Dad had always loved to describe Mom as "the most defiant person I know" was that she was only defiant when it came to defending Dad.

❖ Fifty-Two ❖

When I moved back to New York, it felt like starting my life all over again. The private school where I taught for a year did not renew my contract, despite the valiant efforts of my students, who staged their own sit-in during morning assembly to protest me being let go. I hadn't necessarily wanted to stay, but it was surprisingly difficult to leave. And now I had to figure out what to do with my life.

I didn't want to pursue a career in education or academe, but after my experience at *Elle*, I also felt wary of getting back into magazine journalism. Even with *Sugar in the Raw* due out for publication in January the following year, I certainly would not be able to support myself as a writer or an author of interview books alone. Not anywhere, but definitely not in New York.

So it was a major coup to get an interview with *Charlie Rose* for one of the most prestigious shows on TV—Skip Gates, a regular guest on the *Charlie Rose* show, had given Charlie my name, and put in a good word on my behalf. Charlie was looking for an associate producer, someone with a fresh perspective to help book guests for interviews as well as panel segments about art and culture. I was super excited because I loved TV and the job sounded like a dream.

"I like how you *are*," Charlie said during my interview, over drinks in a dark bar on East 59th Street, across from his penthouse apartment on the Upper East Side.

"Thanks," I said, not really sure what he meant, but also wanting the job so badly I could almost taste it. After doing some research about the show, which I'd never actually watched before Skip suggested me for the job, and learning that it was an interview format, it seemed like the perfect next step and match for me, combining all the things I was good at—writing, interviewing, hosting conversations, looking closely at and interrogating popular culture.

"You're *different*," Charlie said, enunciating the word "different." "I like that. Why don't you come in next week and we'll try it out."

As a writer and associate producer for the *Charlie Rose* show, and without any former television experience beyond my internship at Blackside, I was thrust into the world of one of New York's most celebrated and prestigious cultural institutions. And although I loved it immediately, as with *Elle*, there were no mentors willing to take the time to teach me, no guidelines or formal job description to follow. I led with my interests that I'd shared with Charlie during my interview, and pitched ideas for segments and guests that I thought would bring something unique to the table.

Straight out of the gate, it was clear that Charlie had hired me as a favor to Skip, and he turned on me pretty quickly.

Charlie demanded I book the black guests he wanted but had previously been unable to get, black guests of a perceived level of respectability and intelligence, like Sidney Poitier, while dismissing the black guests I pitched whom he didn't think held the same level of respectability. He constantly accused me of pushing "my own agenda," notably when I pitched panels on hip-hop and the movie *Amistad*, while none of my white colleagues ever seemed to receive criticism for pushing a white agenda when they pitched potential guests and segments.

Charlie also would be openly critical of my work, leaving me increasingly insecure about whatever skill set I had, if any, publicly pointing out errors in my prep work that weren't really errors. For example, the time he insisted that Kris Kristofferson was *not* a Rhodes Scholar.

"This can't be right!" Charlie fumed after doing the first read of my intro as I watched from the control room. "Rebecca! This is ridiculous! Kris Kristofferson is *not* a Rhodes Scholar!"

My gut sank, and my face got hot. Luckily Kristofferson wasn't in the studio at the time. Charlie often prerecorded his intros. The senior producer standing next to me rushed out onto the set in a panic, grabbed the blue prep pages, crossed some things out, and handed it back to Charlie, then quickly retyped the intro into the teleprompter. He read it again without the Rhodes Scholar part.

Later I went back over my research and sources. We had the internet by then, if not Google, and I found where I'd read about the Rhodes Scholarship. In fact, Kristofferson *did* earn a Rhodes Scholarship to study literature at Oxford in London in 1958.

So while I loved the job of booking and writing notes, meeting and talking to guests, working for Charlie was miserable.

I held on to the better moments for dear life. It was part of the job to greet guests in the green room, specifically the guests whose segments you were producing, and then see them out after they'd recorded their conversations with Charlie. There were several memorable moments with guests as I waited with them for the elevator doors to open and take them down to the lobby, including the time I asked Quentin Tarantino why he seemed to be so obsessed with black people, and he said, "Because black people are awesome!"

Another time Fran Lebowitz openly bemoaned the fact that I hadn't been at a party for Toni Morrison she assumed Charlie would have mentioned to me. "Why weren't you there? I expected you there," Fran said, in her clipped, acerbic way. She was appalled when I told her that Charlie hadn't said anything to me about it, especially since Toni Morrison had just been on the show. Even as I was the only black producer on staff, the only black woman, also the author of three interview-based books, two of which were about black writers and writing, Charlie would not let me produce the segment with Morrison. When I asked him directly why he had assigned it to another producer, Charlie said I wasn't ready, and that he needed someone "good" on this one.

I brought to work with me three of my Toni Morrison books the day she came to record her interview with Charlie—*Beloved*, *The Bluest Eye*, and, of course, *Sula*. I approached her in the green room, where, astonished to be in her presence, I told her how much she and her work had meant to me and presented the books, each of which she signed, *With Pleasure, Toni Morrison*.

She was the living ancestor I'd been waiting for.

✦ Fifty-Three ✦

"*Remember, you said you'd do this* for me," Mateo said, sitting on a tall bar stool, having just watched me hang his stick figure on a napkin for failing to get the eight-letter title for a John Carpenter film.

"And only for you," I said, giving him my biggest of big-sister looks. "You're up." I flipped my napkin to the blank side and slid it over to him, trying not to think about the dinner I'd agreed to have with him and Tess a few days later.

"When was the last time you two saw each other?"

"I don't know, a while. Maybe a year? We've emailed, though," I said, looking at the blank napkin, waiting for him to draw out the gallows for my stick figure's neck. "It hasn't been good."

I was specifically thinking of Tess's last email to me, after the suicide of writer Michael Dorris, when his adopted daughter, one of several adopted children he had with the novelist Louise Erdrich, claimed he had sexually abused her. Tess reiterated her belief that Dad was the source of my trauma, while also suggesting Joe had somehow mistreated me, even though I'd told her next to nothing about our meeting three years before.

Rebecca,

I am not suggesting an extreme act of incest on anyone's part. I am suggesting that your place as daughter-girlchild in your growing was not always that clear—there is a broad arc of incestuous / inappropriate behaviors in families. And I respect your experience, but I think, given my place and interest in you, I see some things different. . . . I know what I have seen, been told, what I intuit—I have that—and just can't surf over that truth.

I feel you have been treated inappropriately by both your fathers and what makes me sad is that you blame yourself. . . . Like most charismatic men, David C's ego has been unwieldy at times. I do believe that he loves you, that he would never knowingly hurt you, and that he thinks of you as emphatically beautiful (though I will never understand the relevance of your knowing this and being regularly reminded of it by your male parent—it is the least important, most shallow human attribute).

Your mother, as you state so wishfully in your dedication, was never fierce during the years after I met you. I think we both wish she were.

The dedication Tess was referring to is in *Sugar in the Raw*, which I dedicated to both Mom and Dad, but especially to Mom, who, I wrote, *raised a black girlchild in America on sheer conviction and fierce motherlove.* I maintain this to be true, but it is also true that Mom's ferocity shifted and waned after my reunion with Tess, as she and Dad leaned further into being interesting people rather than attentive parents.

"I wish you two would just get over it, and go back to loving each other. How hard is that?"

Hard, but I didn't say that to Mateo. For some time, he and I had been very good at keeping our agreement to not discuss Tess, in particular my relationship with her. But it was hard for Mateo to be both her son and my brother while she and I were in such precarious flux after fifteen years of having been so close. Tess was coming to visit him at his new place in Brooklyn, and Mateo asked me to join them for dinner as a favor.

We went to a Thai restaurant in Mateo's neighborhood; he and Tess were already there when I arrived. There were polite hugs and hellos, awkward laughter and palpable tension. Tess looked well, a couple of graying hairs and a few more wrinkles, but the same pretty hazel eyes and soft, delicate lips. We were looking over the menus, Tess asked about Charlie and remarked on how interesting my job must be, when Mateo suddenly blurted out, "Yeah, *really* interesting. She's having dinner with that actor from *Roc*, Charles Dutton, next week." I felt like smacking him with my menu, but instead just glared at him.

"Well," Tess said, before I had a chance to say anything, "Charles Dutton is an ex-con."

"That is so typical of you," I said, feeling my fury start to spike.

"Oh calm down, Rebecca," Tess said, folding her menu and placing it on the table, as if she'd been needlessly interrupted.

"And let me guess, next you're going to remind me how many black men you've dated, right?"

"I'm sorry I said anything! Can you guys stop?!" Mateo suddenly looked so young to me. It broke my heart how much this dinner had mattered to him, and that I'd probably already fucked it up.

"Let's just eat," I said, preemptively shutting myself down before Tess did.

We ate pad thai and dumplings, sticky rice and chicken skewers, and talked about the pending holidays and other things as diplomatically as possible. I left them both after dinner and immediately went to a bar to get drunk.

Fifty-Four

Charlie fired me after two years. "I can't keep carrying you while you try to launch your writing career," he said. I was paid an annual salary of $38,000 for what was often a sixty-hour workweek, in a hostile, racist, and misogynistic environment where my aptitude and intelligence were constantly questioned; if that constitutes being carried, then we need to talk about what "carrying" someone means.

Several months after the release of *Sugar in the Raw*, which had garnered the best reviews of my book-writing career, an agent from a well-established literary agency reached out and offered to poach me from Lila, who had her own independent boutique agency, with the promise of getting me a six-figure advance for a memoir if I'd agree to write it as a direct response to Tess's book. I thought about it, and even drafted a proposal, every sentence of which felt forced, contrived. But I wasn't ready, and moreover, I didn't want to write a direct response to Tess's book.

What I really wanted was to write screenplays, and so when Tess came back to me for the fifth time in five years about signing off on the movie rights to her book, I put a very big bluffing chip on the table, and she called it. The only way I'd agree to sign off on the film rights was if I wrote the adapted screenplay.

"I just want to go to the Emmys," Tess said. "So do a good job."

The deal with Hallmark paid me a flat fee of $50,000, and gave me membership into the Writers Guild of America. I moved into my third loft in New York, second in Brooklyn, this one in Gowanus, where I lived by myself, and settled in to spend a year writing a screen adaptation of my life through the lens of my white birth mother, who had consistently manipulated my emotions and erased my blackness, sabotaged nearly every meaningful relationship I'd ever had with a black man throughout my life, and suggested that my white adoptive father had molested me as a child. What could possibly go wrong?

That was the year I started drinking whiskey. And martinis. I'd work all day, reading passages from Tess's book, hearing her voice saying them, trying to write cinematic scenes that didn't break my heart, and then stop in the evenings, pour myself a glass of whiskey neat, and try to forget what I'd been reading all day. Up until then, I'd been a fairly strict wine drinker, but this enterprise called for something stronger, even though I didn't really like the taste of whiskey. Other nights after writing, I'd go to a bar and drink martinis, which also weren't that tasty to me, until I started to slur, chatting it up with the bartender or whoever else might be sitting next to me.

Almost everything I read in Tess's book made me want to inflict more pain on myself, just to keep it going. I started to bring home random men I'd met at whatever bar where I'd been drinking, tempting fate, just waiting to pick the wrong one, enacting the self-fulfilling prophecy I knew all along would one day play itself out. If I didn't meet anyone to bring home with me, I'd take a cab or walk home, and call Mom or Monique or other friends late into the night, desperate for them to help me understand this new and inescapable riddle of agony. I'd wake up hungover and need a few hours before starting the cycle all over again.

It was the first time I'd finished Tess's book all the way through, and then, pretending it was an effort to maintain some semblance of professionalism, I read it again. But I wasn't reading it the second time as a screenwriter; I was reading it as the daughter she used to reconcile herself to her own pain. It was almost surreal how clearly she'd laid it out, how glaringly simple the answer was for why she had been so judgmental and emotionally manipulative to me for all those years. I felt like such a fool.

When Tess discovered she was pregnant with me, she thought having a baby would bring her mother, Lena, back. Lena, who had fled south after spending several months in a Massachusetts institution, told Tess from a pay phone in New Orleans that she would come back to Boston so that they could raise the baby together. Frances gave her blessing, but Roy, the more practical one in the family, thought it was a bad idea. Tess, though, ignored her brother's concerns, and deluded herself into believing that their mother, no longer institutionalized but still mentally ill, was lucid enough to make such a commitment. In the days following, Tess set about knitting baby booties and thinking about names.

"It will be hard to find work," Lena said, in a subsequent phone call to her daughter. "I don't think we can do anything for her." By "her," Lena meant Tess's baby—a girl, Tess had learned at a recent doctor appointment, news she had shared with her mother. Less than a month after she'd made the promise to help raise her granddaughter, Lena resolved that she couldn't do it after all.

Tess had, to use her own word, "extracted" the daughter out of me that she wanted in an effort to replace or replicate the relationship she lost with her mother. It was an extraction that felt as if it had come directly from the marrow of my eleven-year-old bones. I had been unfamiliar to her, so she forced a familiarity, exploited my pliable youth, leveraged my trauma and desperation for her approval, to make a daughter who would function in the same capacity that she did and would have continued to do had her mother not abandoned her. And she'd done it all while dismissing, belittling, or co-opting my blackness.

Tess erased my blackness and then lynched my spirit in an ongoing public spectacle of psychological and emotional violence that started at the Uptown disco club, through to the dean's office at UNH and Elaine's restaurant in New York. I didn't need to kill myself; after reading the book, I felt like I was already dead.

✢ Fifty-Five ✢

"We're very concerned about what's happening in New York," Mom said on the other end of the phone. It was just before nine a.m. on the morning of September 11, 2001, and I'd woken up to the sound of the phone ringing. Otherwise, I never would have been up that early.

"What's going on in New York?" I asked groggily.

"Turn on the TV," she said, with an alarming sense of urgency.

I got out of bed, managing to wrap my comforter around my shoulders with one hand while I kept the phone to my ear with the other.

"OK, hold on," I said, cradling the phone in my shoulder while I grabbed the remote and turned on the TV just in time to see the second plane hit the South Tower. I fell back onto the couch facing the TV in my living room, utterly shocked. "Oh my God, what is happening?"

"Are you OK?" Mom asked, still borderline frantic.

"Yes, Mom. I'm fine."

"Stay inside, but stay on the phone with me."

"What is happening?" That was all I could think to say. And then the phone line cut out. "Mom? Mom?!" I shouted into the receiver, but no one was there anymore.

I sat on the couch all day rocking back and forth, glued to the screen, occasionally trying to call Mom back in New Hampshire, to no avail. By about six p.m., local calls were able to get through, and a friend from my last job at an online company organized a group meetup at a Brooklyn bar that night to process what had happened. I was glad to have a makeshift support system, but I realized, not for the first time, that I had no real community at a time of crisis other than Caryn, who was working for the NYC Department of Education on 9/11, on the ground downtown just blocks from the attacks. Besides Caryn, I didn't really have a community at all.

It wasn't Mom's fault that the phone lines went down during a terrorist attack, but that I was unable to get through to her after she'd called to check in on me was painfully symbolic of how I'd felt my parents had always been with me, especially Mom— intensely loving and present, and then just gone while the world was falling apart around me. I started to think about what I wanted my community to look like and realized that I would have to make it myself.

While I hadn't struggled with my right to choose the abortions I'd had in my early twenties, I often thought about those possible pregnancies as my body maybe trying to tell me what it wanted to do most of all: have a baby. In the weeks following 9/11, when the air was still thick with soot and ash, and everyone in the city ducked like a war vet at the sound of helicopters overhead, I decided that saving money and getting to a place where I could raise a child on my own would be my main priority moving forward. And that meant upping my hustle game, which was already pretty demanding.

For the next three years, I worked a series of freelance writing and teaching jobs, hosted a show for WNET about the post–9/11 generation, and sold another book proposal, this one for a book that would be part interviews, part personal vignettes based on passages from *The Souls of Black Folk,* by W. E. B. Du Bois. I was endlessly sending out résumés for full-time work at online companies or magazines, applying for writing grants and residencies, and cycling through a series of roommates because I could no longer afford to live alone.

While I forged headlong toward my goal to have a baby, I continued to manage the fallout from my break with Tess, who would not take no for an answer. I stopped working on the screenplay, blocked Tess's email address and refused to take her calls; I either returned or burned her letters. At one point I thought it was entirely possible that she might jump out from behind a bush to confront me.

One of the hardest things about breaking things off with Tess was the betrayal Mateo and Sebastian felt, which they let me know about through spates of unleashed vitriol. They told me I was being untrue to myself, that I was weak and pitiful, lacked essence and character. I belonged to the Bancroft family, they said; I was *their* sister, and Tess's daughter. How could I live with myself for turning away from her after all the pain she'd endured after giving me up?

Meanwhile, my relationships with Riana and Sean had also hit a wall. Riana had started calling me late at night, drunk and filled with bitter condemnation. "You think you're so much better than me!" she'd repeat over and over. She was right. I did think I was better than her. Better in that I was making a life for myself that involved a world beyond Warner, where she'd moved back to when her sons, still struggling with their health issues, were about ten.

I read books and magazines, wrote articles, and knew important people, and had conversations about politics and race. I'd confronted my trauma and moved on with my life, while she continued to wallow in her own trauma, and remain willfully ignorant about anything outside of her own small life. Sean had made a fine life for himself, with a successful carpentry business, but remained in Warner, and cultivated the mindset that came along with that choice.

It wasn't just that my siblings and parents didn't see me; it was that they didn't see race or think about blackness, mine or anyone else's, and I felt like I deserved that, at the very least. To be adopted into a white family that did not see or care or think about my blackness or my experience navigating a racist country had always felt lonely and isolating, endlessly confusing, but now it just felt cruel.

✦ Fifty-Six ✦

I was on my way to a **final** interview for a job as editor in chief of a magazine focused on independent film when I dropped a piece of unchewed gum on the subway platform. It was midday on a Friday in late August, and I was not about bullshit that day, self-serious as hell, with my arms crossed over my chest. I'd snapped out a piece of Trident gum, and it fell on the ground. I ignored it, popped out another one, and put it in my mouth.

I'd landed in Greenpoint, Brooklyn, with a roommate after a few years jumping between writing residencies and house-sitting stints, and was on the subway platform in Williamsburg, where you transfer from the G to the L train that takes you into Manhattan. The platform was nearly empty at noon before a long holiday weekend.

"I'll bet you a quarter that between now and the time the train comes, someone will step on that piece of gum you dropped."

Slender and handsome, with level eyes and an understated smile, this white guy who walked up to me on the subway platform felt familiar.

"Um, OK," I said, not entirely sure why I'd agreed to a bet over something so stupid. We stood side by side, his shoulders not too much taller than mine, staring down at the small, white tab of gum as a few people walked by, their feet just nearly missing it. After a few minutes, we heard the rumble of the train coming out of the dark tunnel from the left, and as it pulled up in front of us, someone stepped on the gum.

We got on the train, and I paid him his due quarter. He was carrying an overnight bag as we stood holding the pole between us, and I asked him if he was going away for the weekend.

"Actually," he said plainly, "I'm headed up to Harvard for a conference on race and social policy."

I waited for him to go on about all the black friends he had, or indicate in some way that he deserved praise or a reward for being a white guy who went to conferences about race. But no, that was all, just a white guy going to a conference about race, as if he was on his way to the grocery store for a loaf of bread.

"Do you live around here?" I asked, because now I was intrigued.

"Yeah, I just got back from Berkeley, where I was doing a postdoc. I'm living in Greenpoint."

"Me, too! I'm living in Greenpoint, too, and actually I did a fellowship at Harvard—is your conference at the Du Bois Institute?"

"No, but that's cool. We should get a drink sometime."

"Sure, yeah. I'm Rebecca," I said.

"I'm Chris," he responded, unselfconscious, though not especially laid back either. There was an ease about him that seemed transcendent but also grounded, genuinely curious but not nearly as self-serious as I was. I gave him my card, which he took, and as he got off the train first, he said, "I'll give you a call."

Suddenly I didn't trust him or the exchange, the serendipity or unlikelihood of it. What were the chances of meeting a handsome white guy on the subway platform who seems perfectly lovely, not weird or presumptuous, who cares enough about race to go to a whole conference on the subject but not make a big deal about it? This guy was never going to call me.

"Yeah," I said, back to the self-serious, ain't-about-that-bullshit mode I'd been in when he first walked up and immediately disarmed me. "You do that."

He looked at me bewildered, but smiled anyway. The subway doors closed, and I went to my job interview. Chris called on Sunday night when he'd returned from the conference and invited me to dinner the following Thursday.

In a cozy restaurant on Houston Street on the Lower East Side of Manhattan, we'd just been seated and hadn't even ordered drinks when I said, "Listen, I'm having a baby by the time I'm thirty-six, so what do you want out of this?" I was thirty-four years old.

Chris smiled, unfazed, and said, "Maybe let's have dinner first?"

We had dinner first, then we got pregnant, and then we got married. I was seven months pregnant with our son at our wedding in April 2005, a month before I turned thirty-six.

In the seventeen years since Chris and I first got together, as we've seen the country become more racially divisive than it was during my childhood, it has become resolutely clear to me that I only could have married a white man who is also a scholar of race and American history (and a former DJ with dope taste in music). Someone willing to immerse himself in the structural and racial disparities that have existed for time immemorial, who understands, because he's taken the time to read and research, that black history is American history, and that there are a million different black stories and histories that have never been told by design.

For the average white person in America, even and perhaps especially the average white liberal person who thinks they are on the right side of racial issues, the privilege is too entrenched. The work and humility required to fully understand systemic racism in this country holds no realistic appeal. Most white people go straight to their own sense of guilt and then don't know how to manage their feelings from there, as we've seen play out over and over again in the "woke" era of 2020.

It's as if the only way for white people to become conversant in issues of racism and racial injustice is to make it their full-time job, which is maybe not such a bad idea?

It has been critically important to me that Chris, as a white man, understands how dearly I hold onto my own blackness, but equally important that he understand how necessary it is that our son be encouraged to hold onto his blackness, too.

✦ Epilogue ✦

For years during my twenties, I tacitly memorialized the version of me from a fictionalized world created by the white gaze with photos of myself as a little girl on the walls of my various homes—clad in a purple-and-green bikini wearing sunglasses and sitting on a yellow banana-seat bike, emerging from the water with wet droplets falling from my afro, wearing a flowy scarf around my neck and a straw hat and striking a mysterious pose.

I took most of them down as I got older, but there was one that I kept up after my son, Kofi, was born, of me when I was about four years old. In it, I'm holding a frog that I'd caught in the brook near our house on Pumpkin Hill, and I am grinning from ear to ear, my brown face alight, afro wild, eyes delighted.

The photo was on the wall in the longish stretch of hallway opposite the kitchen in our second apartment as a family together. Kofi, who was born less than two years after Chris and I met on the subway platform in Brooklyn, learned to walk by pushing a little plastic cart up and down that hallway, passing the photo, which was too high up on the wall for him to see. One day, when he was about four years old himself, he looked up and saw the picture, and then turned to me and said, "Mommy, why I'm holding a frog?"

In the sound of his small, sweet voice, I heard what I'd been waiting to hear my entire life: this boy, with his tiny brown fingers grasping the handle of his little cart, eyes deep brown and bright, loose curls reaching up and around his tender, curious face—this boy saw himself in me.

Years later, when Kofi was about seven, he and I arrived for our annual summer visit to my parents in New Hampshire ahead of Chris, who would join us after he finished his summer advising work. We were out for breakfast with Mom and Dad at a busy local restaurant and were looking at our menus when Kofi leaned over to me and quietly whispered, genuinely mystified, "Mom, why is everyone here white?"

When I was my son's age, this wall-to-wall whiteness, which he looked at with discerning and culturally sophisticated, city-born eyes, was all I knew, and although I took some comfort in Kofi's bafflement, I wanted Mom and Dad to account for their choice to raise me there, to my black son, directly. "Ask your grandparents," I said.

"Because many of the people who live here are descendants of the first settlers to the area—those who worked and farmed the land for their livelihood," Dad responded. "And the first settlers were white." Without needing a prompt to answer further, he said, "As a naturalist, I need to feel connected to whatever undeveloped land there is left."

It had only ever been about him and what *he* needed. I didn't want to make a scene in the restaurant—already people were looking at me and Kofi, the only two black people there—but I felt enraged anew through the keen reflection of my son. A rage that has only continued to blaze years on.

A few weeks after that visit with my parents, Michael Brown was fatally shot in the back by police in the streets of Ferguson,

Missouri. This time, Kofi asked me, while we sat at the kitchen table together in our apartment, "Are you gonna get shot, Mom? Am *I* gonna get shot? Because we're black?"

I explained that yes, there was a chance that some white people might want to shoot us because we are black, because American history has not been kind to us, and that we, black folks, and especially young black boys, are left with the burden of fear that we might be in the wrong place at the wrong time.

"We were never supposed to be here. Or to survive. But we *are* here and we *have* survived, and you, Kofi, can look to that legacy of survival and resilience and beauty and strength as your own," I said, echoing the same sentiments that inform what has become my life's work—writing and talking about black culture in America, amplifying black voices, and holding up the narrative of black folks both collectively and as individuals.

Kofi got out of his chair and came to sit on my lap, his nine-year-old self still small enough to curl into my body, though just barely, and we sat together for a little while without talking. I breathed in the smell of his hair and skin, absorbed the glorious weight of his need for my love, for the safety he found in my arms—for his need for *me*. It was bittersweet, not just because of the subject matter that had prompted this moment, but also because I thought of my birth father and felt a wave of sadness take over me.

The year before, a friend of Joe's had found me online and called to tell me that Joe had died of complications from diabetes and kidney failure, among other things. Joe did not have health insurance or access to proper health care, and subsequently did not survive as a black man in America. I thought there would be more time, but now Kofi will never meet or know his black birth grandfather, and that will always be one of my deepest regrets.

÷ ÷

My son is light-skinned black. In the summertime when he was little, his skin, like mine when I was a child, turned toasty brown. My parents, his white grandparents, thought he was beautiful, especially during the darker-skinned season, and said so often. But as he got older, when his inflection started to match his skin tone and he chose to wear his hair in a style modeled after his favorite black basketball players, I saw a shift in the way my parents viewed him. As his own sense of blackness began to take shape, Mom and Dad didn't quite know how to interact with him.

On one of our last Christmas visits to New Hampshire a few years ago, Dad tripped inelegantly over his understanding of Kwanzaa—"I mean, every day is Kwanzaa, right? Hey, it's OK, it's Kwanzaa! But you guys know that already!" It felt like he was mocking the holiday traditionally celebrated by black families, and thereby mocking us. On our drive home to Brooklyn, Kofi asked why there was seemingly no evidence in their house that they had raised a black child. No black art, books, or music, like there was in our home.

"I mean, it's all, like, turtles," he said from the back seat. "Does that hurt your feelings, Mom?"

"A little," I said, looking over toward Chris in the driver's seat, hoping he could help me out here in explaining white people to his son.

"Yeah, I mean," Chris began, "I think Gramma-Rette and Grampa-Dave are fairly representative of most white people of their generation living in a small, rural town."

"But shouldn't they care more because Mom is black?" Kofi asked.

"In a best-case scenario," Chris said, "yes."

"So it wasn't a best-case scenario, Mom?"

"Nope. Not so much," I said, and folded the window visor down to block the glare of an early-morning winter sun on a long stretch of rural highway.

⊹ Acknowledgments ⊹

M_y *literary agent, Maria Massie, is* one of the most gracious readers and editors I've ever worked with. And that's before she even put on her agent hat. Thank you, Maria, for your generous and rigorous work in helping me to shape the proposal for this book, and then taking it out into the publisher bidding wars and fighting for it like a badass.

Thank you to Christine Pride for choosing this book and guiding it through so smartly and with such heart, patience, and clarity. And to Hana Park and Priscilla Painton for such a seamless handoff to the finish.

Thank you to Megan Carpentier, my editor during the two years I was a columnist at the *Guardian*—you made me a better writer. You just did.

Thanks to my former colleagues at WNYC—you wonderfully weird and wild troupe of journalists, creatives, podcasters, talkers, and listeners.

Thank you to Crissle West and Kid Fury for *The Read*, which kept the sound of black joy and laughter and mess in my ear during my regular runs.

No writer, living or dead, has influenced me more than Toni Morrison—I could not, and likely would not, have written this memoir if not for the resolute beauty of her peerless scope and skill as a writer, her regal existence as a black woman who loved her blackness and her womanness beyond measure, and her unyielding belief in the power and practice of *doing* language.

Thank you to early readers and generous friends Kate Hinds, Trista Schroeder, Gina Prince-Bythewood, Nicole Cliffe, Cindi Lieve, Pam Koffler, Christine Vachon, and Anna Holmes. So grateful for the continued love and support from Davira Jimenez, Dorlan Kimbrough, Negar Ahkami, Randy Dottin, Bo Mehrad, Liz Dwyer, Peter Kane, Lisa Forero, Amissa Miller, and Karen Frillman.

To my day ones—Leah Giberson, Rebecca Emeny, Monique Cormier, Sarah MacMillin, Caryn Rivers, and Michael Ladd— y'all are squad and I love you.

And a special thank-you to you Caryn Rivers for coming into my life at the exact moment that you did, and for letting me choose you and Anwar as the extended black family I always needed and am now so lucky to have in you both.

Thank you Renny, for your sweet, fierce devotion to family and staying connected.

Joe Banks—I wish we'd had more time, and that the world had done better by you.

Thank you Mom and Dad for modeling the integrity it takes to create and stay true to your own set of values and beliefs. And also for your great love. Thank you Riana for your beautiful heart and unbowed bravery, and for allowing me to share part of your deeply personal story in these pages. Thank you Sean for your quiet, steadfast loyalty.

Chris, my love. Thank you for all of it.

And Kofi, there is nothing and no one more magnificent than you.

✤ About the Author ✤

REBECCA CARROLL is a writer, creative consultant, and host of the podcast *Come Through with Rebecca Carroll: 15 essential conversations about race in a pivotal year for America*. Previously, she was a cultural critic at WNYC and a critic-at-large for the *Los Angeles Times*, and her essays and criticism have appeared in the *Atlantic*, the *New York Times*, *Ebony*, *Essence*, the *Guardian*, and *New York* magazine, among many other publications. She is the author of several books about race in America, including the award-winning *Sugar in the Raw: Voices of Young Black Girls in America*. She lives in Brooklyn with her husband and teenage son.